MW01618549

SHARON LATHAN

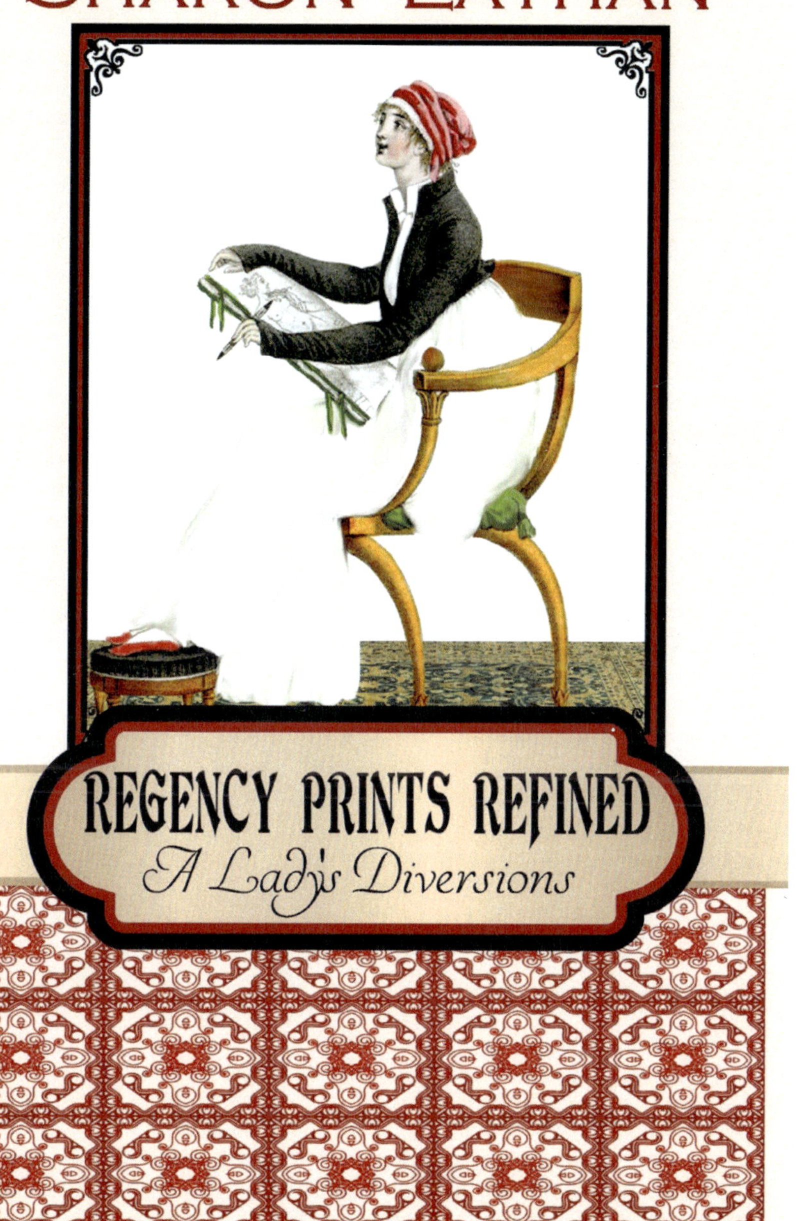

Published by Sharon Lathan
TSBO Publications
www.SharonLathanAuthor.com

ISBN: 099161061X
ISBN-13: 978-0991610617

INTRODUCTION

In the centuries before photography, capturing a visual image to share with others or preserve for posterity was dependent upon skilled craftsmen. Whether sculpting stone, painting upon canvas, carving wood, drawing on paper, or any of the myriad techniques employed, the artist was key.

Museums, private collectors, and libraries all over the world secure the treasures of the past. While some of these treasures are better able to withstand the passage of time, far too many do not fare so well. If saved from destruction in the first place, printed materials are especially fragile, and rapidly decay even when properly preserved. Regency Era fashion prints (or "plates"), and engraved drawings of daily life and amusements, fall into the latter category.

Thankfully, the vast majority of published prints have survived, and digitalized versions of these prints are easily accessed via the web. A surprising quantity of the original prints (and thus their digitalized copies) are in terrific condition. Most show some evidence of time with colors faded and yellowed paper marked by creases, water damage, smudges, tears, and so on. Then there are those prints severely deteriorated, particularly those not initially of the highest quality.

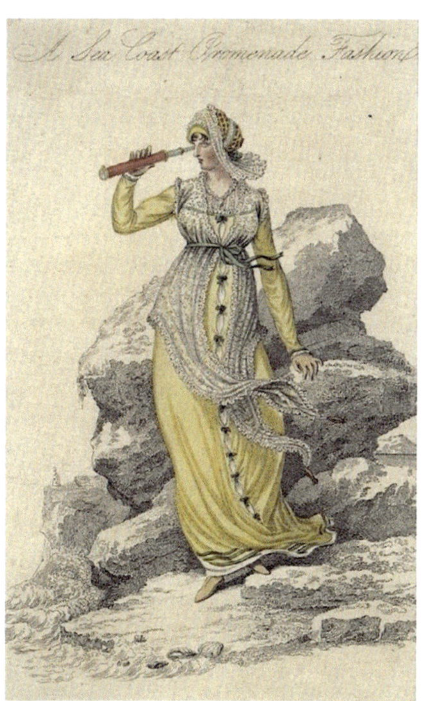

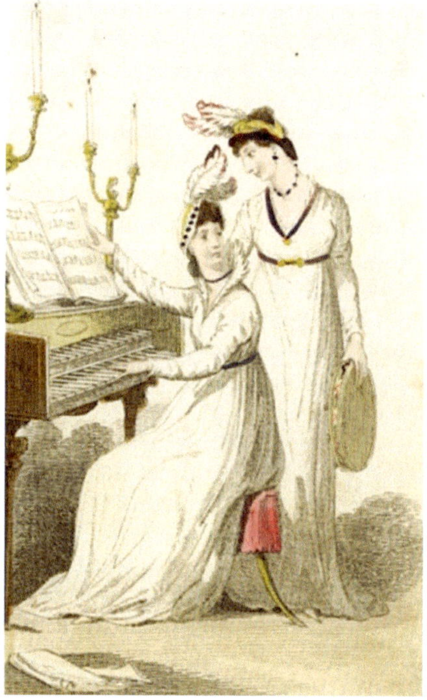

Like so many people today, I admit to being a Pinterest addict. In the beginning my interest in Pinterest was focused on promotion of, and research for, my novels. My boards on cinema, the 1980s, and Disneyland came later! Visual imagery of period clothing, objects, and locations are vital for a historical novelist. Pinterest is the best website to begin an image search, with the "related pins" and embedded links augmenting the hunt for images and supplementary information.

The more pictures I pinned, the more boards I created to organize them. One of the 70 boards I currently have is dedicated to "Regency Fashion Plates & Drawings."

It was this collection of 400+ fashion plates — and my skills in digital design — that prompted me to volunteer to tackle a project for the 2015 Jane Austen Society of North America (JASNA) Annual General Meeting (AGM) hosted by the Greater Louisville JASNA Region, of which I am a proud member. Coordinators Bonny Wise and Alana Gillett wanted to decorate the luncheon and banquet tables with Regency prints specifically depicting people engaged in activities of some sort, as per the 2015 AGM theme "Living in Jane Austen's World."

I was happy to take on the task, but never dreamed the simple behest to re-size and polish twenty-five plates for 5x7 framed photos would lead where it did. Before I finished the AGM project I had accumulated over 650 prints on my Pinterest board, and refurbished 105 plates for Bonny and Alana to choose from!

Now when I look at a print from the 1790s to 1820s I envision how fantastic it *could look,* and itch to open my GIMP program. The process of restoring color and enhancing with modern computer magic is a delightful pastime I plan to continue. I have discovered a new passion!

Nonetheless, I was saddened by the fact that the 105 superbly reimagined prints resembling weeks of painstaking work were left to languish in a computer folder. No one, other than the JASNA AGM attendees in October of 2015, would ever see them. Oh, the tragedy! Worse yet, without a legitimate purpose, how could I justify wasting time on indulging my new passion?

Unless…

An idea was borne. How about a series of full-color photo books? Each one could have a theme, contain a bit of history and fashion descriptions, be modestly sized and priced, and above all be a captivating addition to a Regency lovers library. Fabulous idea!

Owing to the AGM theme, it was logical for the first book to contain those prints of Regency women engaged in daily activities. Hence, ***A Lady's Diversions*** as the title.

Then there was the series title to decide upon. "Regency Prints" was easy, but why "refined"?

I searched the thesaurus for words to describe what I had done to these old prints. Restore, recover, refurbish, repair, renew, revive… The list was long, but it was the definition of "refined" that appealed to me.

Refined : 1) having well-bred taste, as in *refined people*; 2) to purify from what is coarse or debasing; 3) to bring to a finer state, as in *refined sugar*; 4) to become more fine, elegant, polished, or precise.

That is what I do! I take what was once perfection but has over time been damaged, and not just erase the ruin but restore to a finer state than the original! My goal has been to remain as close to the essence of the original print as possible, while employing modern graphics, textures, and photographic images to enhance.

Additionally, each picture has been created for photo printing and framing. Along with this book — and the ones I hope will follow — each image has been added to my Image Gallery for purchase in a vast array of photo print options and sizes, as cards singly or in packs, to place on a mug or tote, and much more.

Visit my website : www.SharonLathanAuthor.com for the link to purchase prints, or go directly to : www.sharonlathan-imagegallery.com/Regency-Prints-Refined

Thank you for purchasing this book. Read on, and please enjoy!

Sincerely, Sharon Lathan

A Lady's Diversions

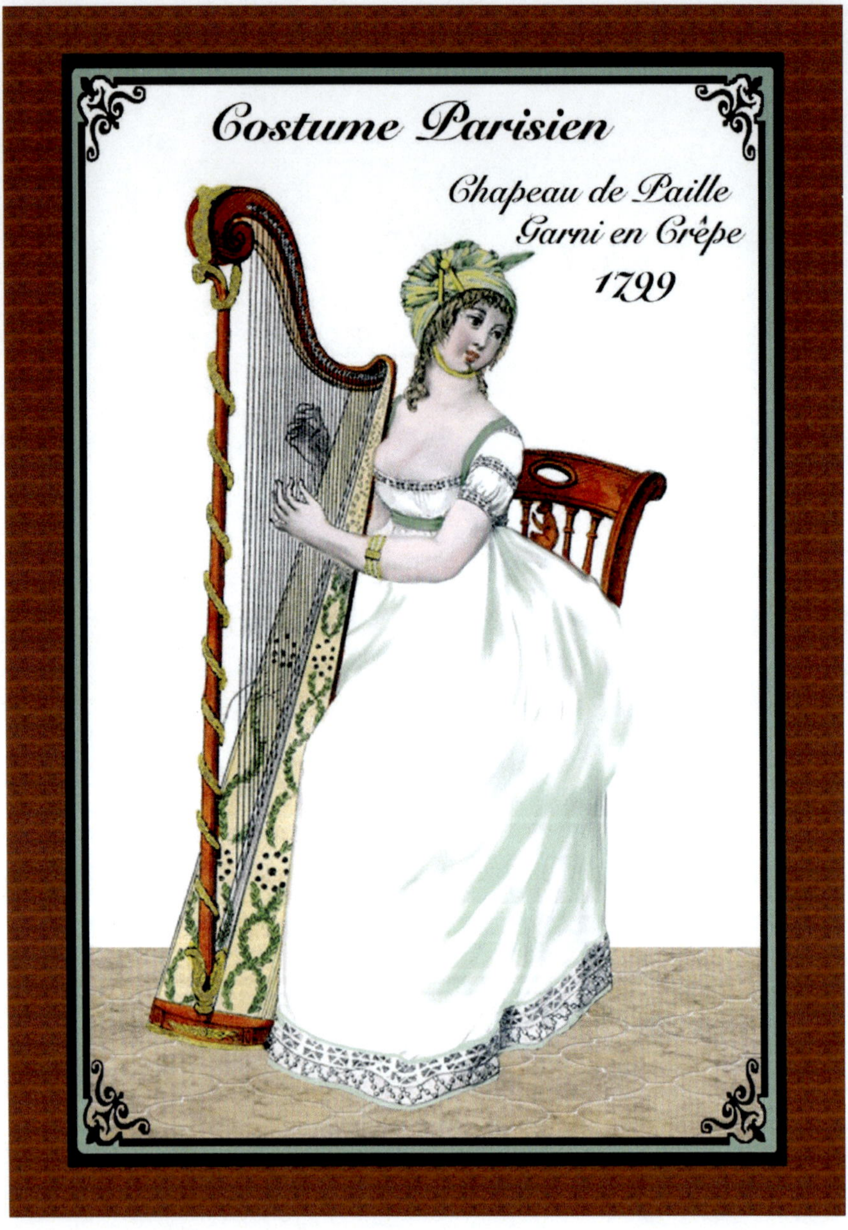

Costume Parisien

Chapeau de Paille
Garni en Crêpe
1799

Plate 1

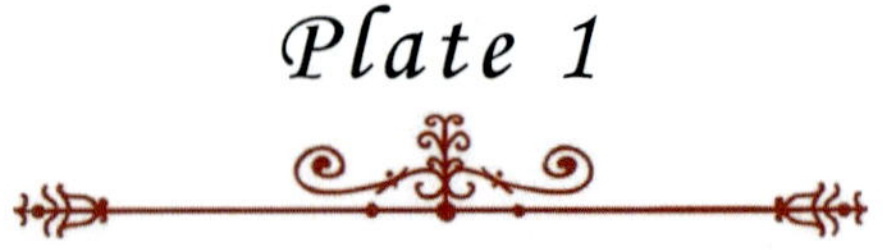

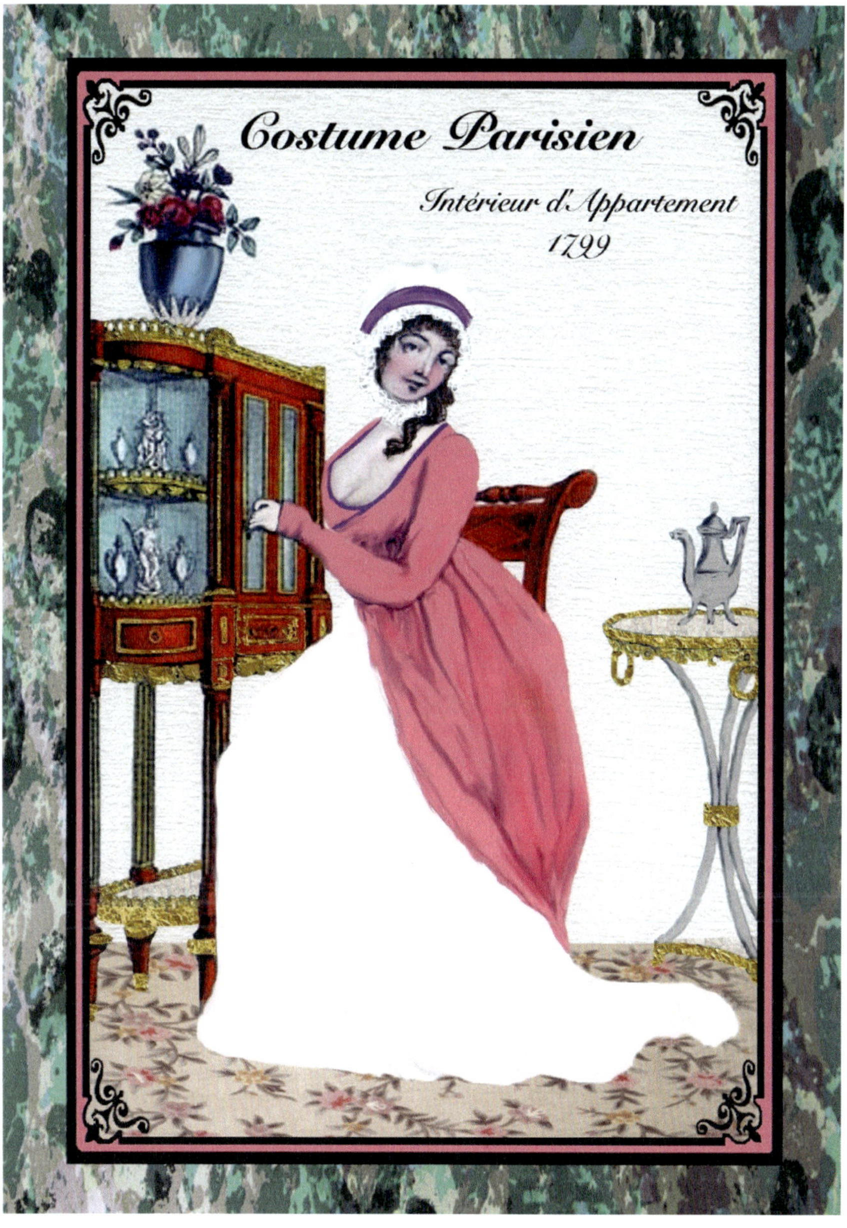

Costume Parisien

Intérieur d'Appartement
1799

Plate 2

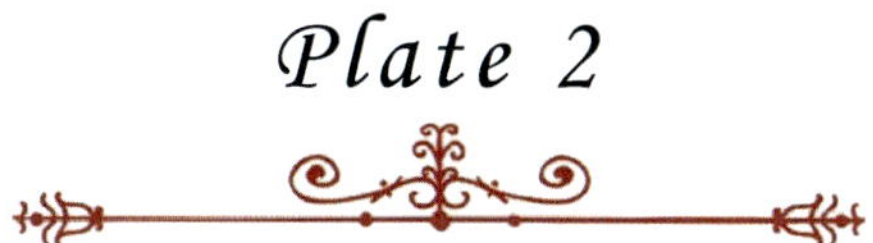

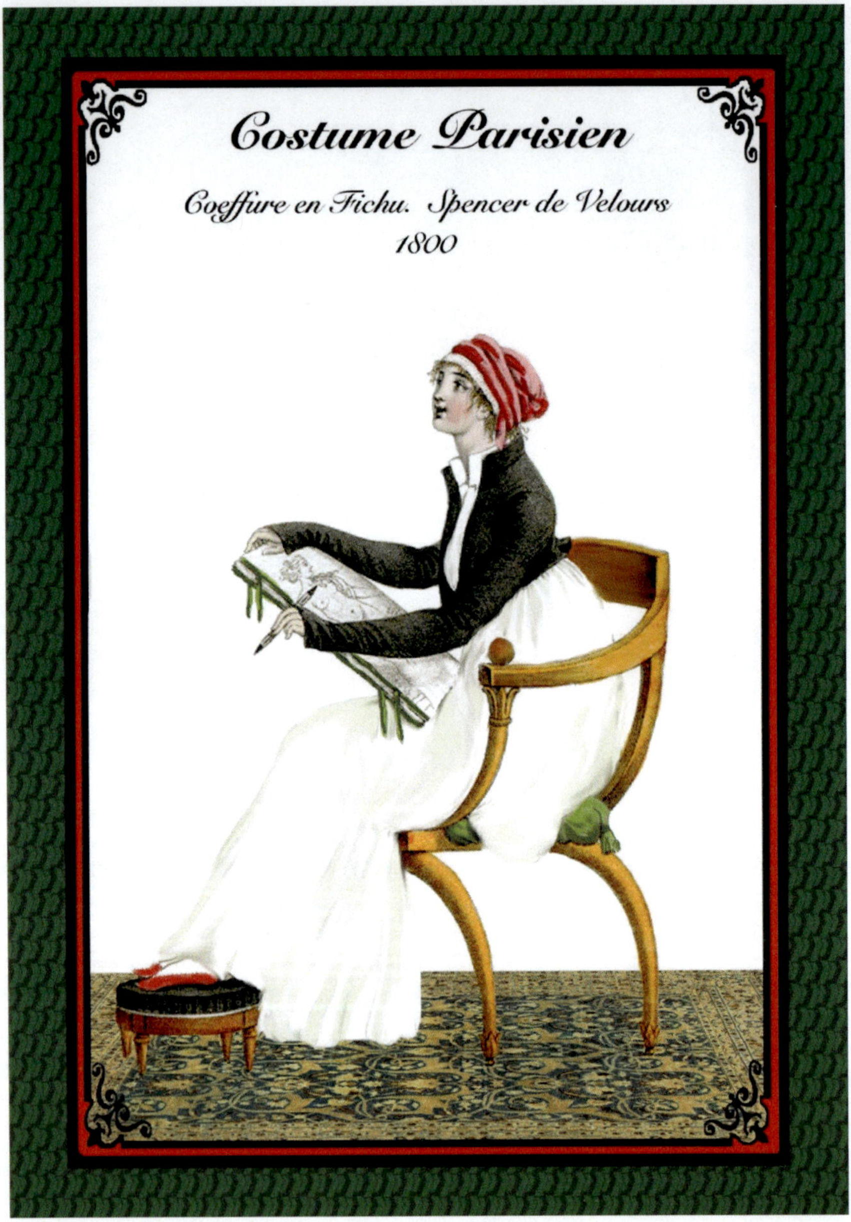

Costume Parisien

Coeffure en Fichu. Spencer de Velours
1800

Plate 3

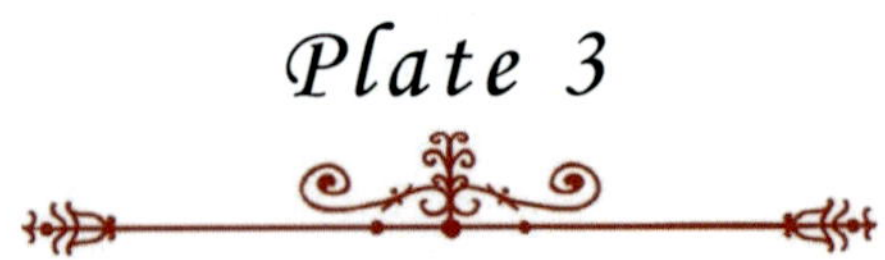

Plate 1 :

A woman playing a gorgeous pedal harp (also known as a concert harp). These types of harps were designed primarily for classical music. The pedal mechanism changed the pitches of the strings, and were first used in 1687.

Clearly this is an original French fashion plate as no British dress would expose the bosom to this degree. Sexy! Scant is left to the imagination, is there?

Translation of the French caption: "Straw hat trimmed in crepe" with *chapeau* = *hat*. Crepe is a thin, nearly transparent silk gauze, and while noted as the fabric trimming the turban-styled hat, it isn't a stretch to consider it might also be the dress fabric.

Plate 2 :

A beautiful lady sitting beside her curio cabinet.

Translation of the French caption: "Inside apartment" as an indication that the viewer is glimpsing an intimate, private scene. Like Plate #1, this gown is a bit more daring than the typical English dress. She is in morning attire, her night cap in place, and a simple open gown over her dress. Gowns tended to be fuller at this point in fashion history.

Plate 3 :

A woman artist sketching a female nude. She is gazing upward, presumably at the stone statue she is drawing. Fascinating!

Translation of the French caption: *Coeffure* is an older spelling of *coiffure*, both meaning "hair, or hairstyle." Fichu refers to a thin, rectangular scarf typically worn for modesty over the shoulders and tucked into the bodice. In this print, *fichu* is referring to the scarf covering her hair.

Spencer de Velour is literally a Spencer jacket made of velour, a velvet-like fabric typically spun from wool.

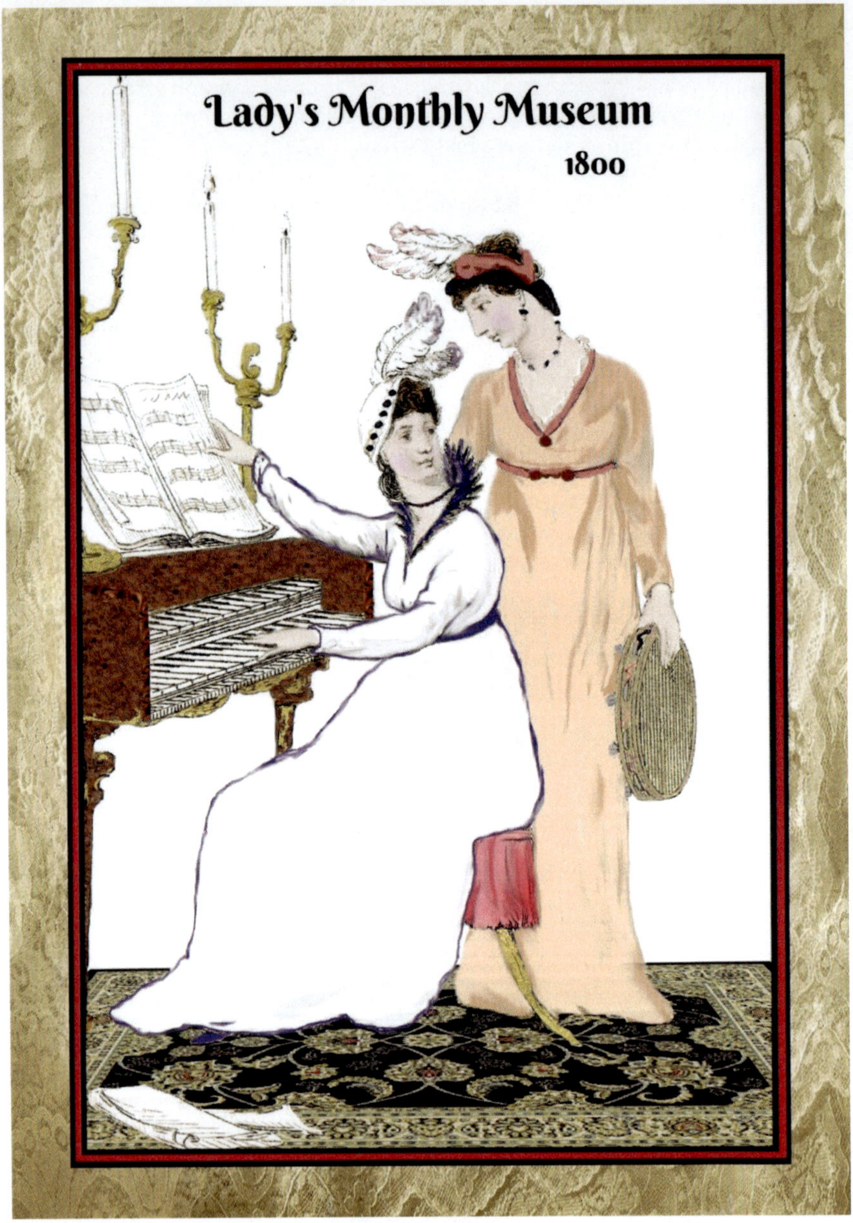

Lady's Monthly Museum

1800

Plate 4

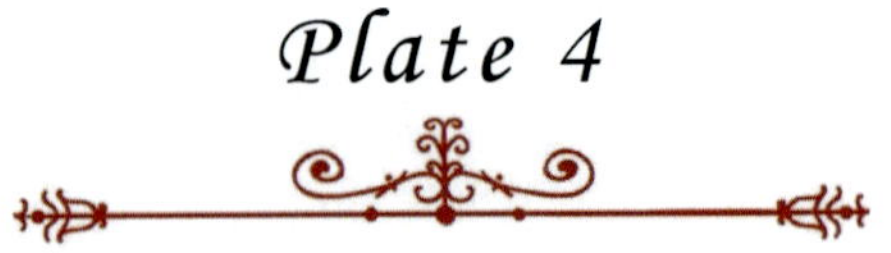

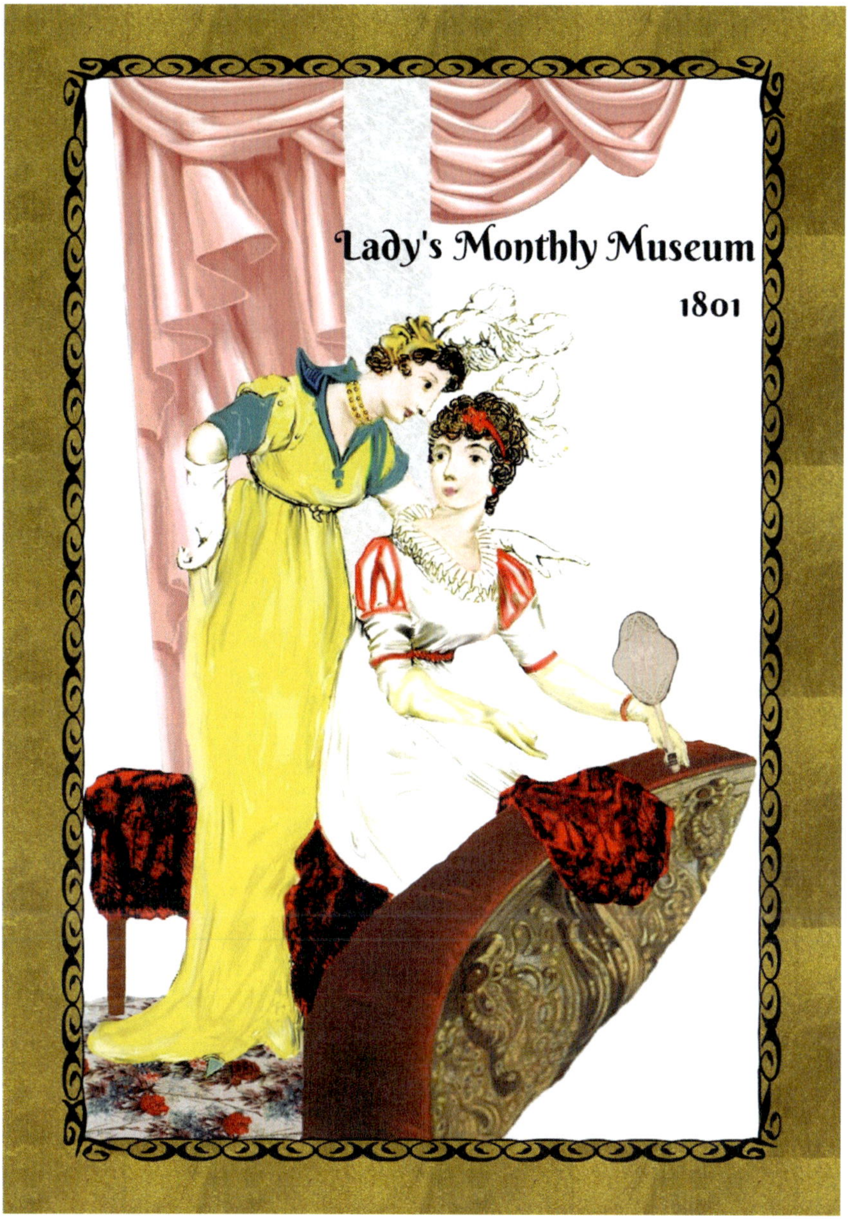

Lady's Monthly Museum

1801

Plate 5

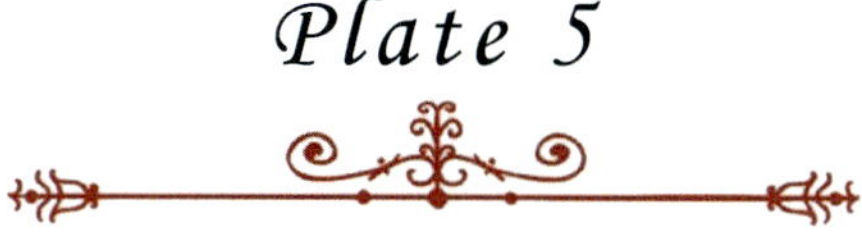

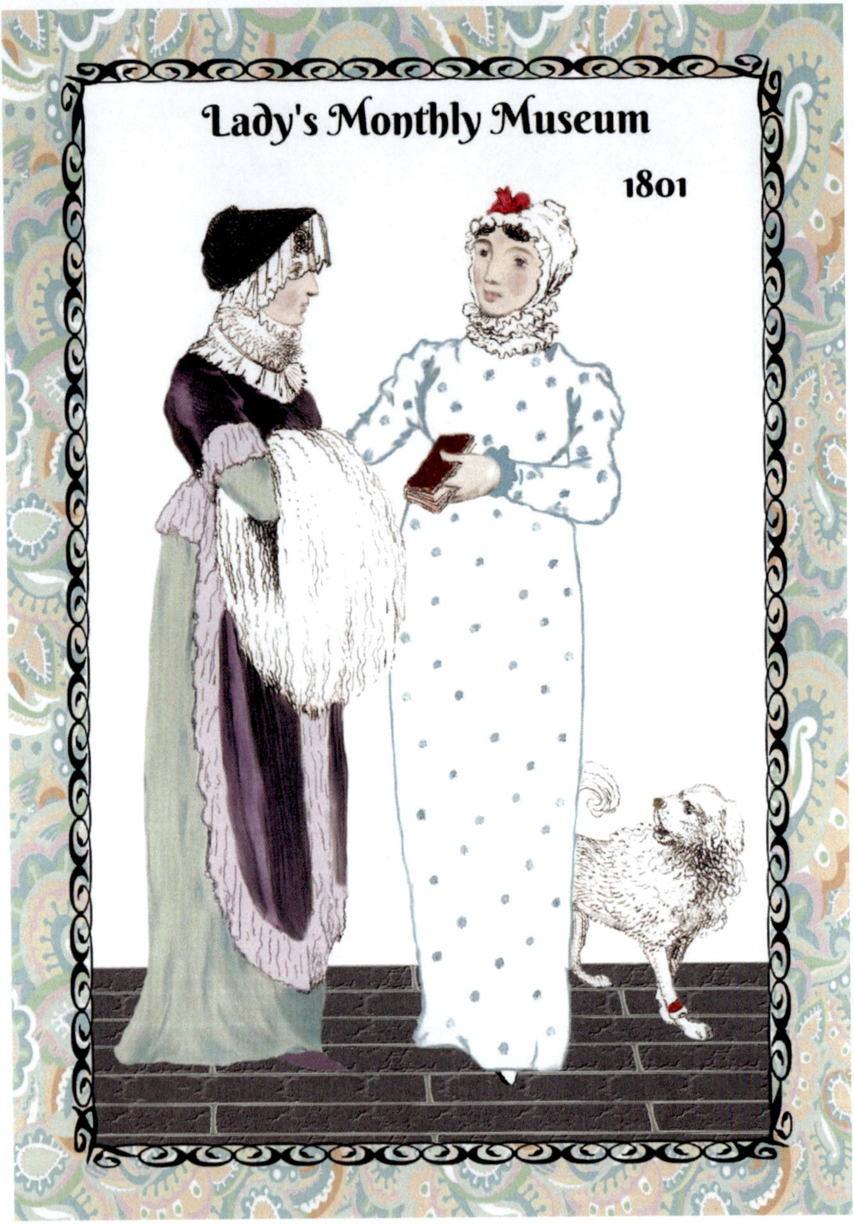

Lady's Monthly Museum

1801

Plate 6

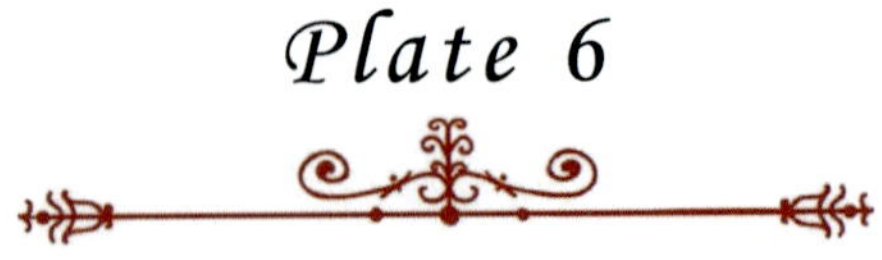

Plate 4 :

One lady holds a tambourine and stands behind a second lady sitting before a harpsichord. The combination is fascinating. The tambourine has been around for centuries, yet somehow seems an odd accompaniment to the keyboards. Interestingly, Mozart was the earliest western composer to write music for a tambourine, and by the late-18th century the instrument was common in an orchestra's percussion section. I learned something new with this print!

Lady's Monthly Museum magazine was the least expensive of the many women's magazines, and the drawings were typically of a lower quality. In this instance the original was a simple line drawing with few colors added. I enhanced with gold leaf and wood texture, as well as colorizing, while maintaining the essence of the original.

Plate 5 :

Two ladies chatting while awaiting a theatrical performance to commence.

Another *Lady's Monthly Museum* print. Notice the similarity in composition to Plate #4. Of interest here are the loose fitting gloves, over which the sitting lady has placed a bracelet, and the seated lady's "ruff" collar. Ruffs — wide pleated collars stiffened with starch or wire — were popular from the late 1400s to the mid-1600s. Think Shakespeare and Queen Elizabeth I. It is a rare fashion design for this era. Feathers, on the other hand, as in the impressive ostrich plumes both ladies have adorning their hair, were a fashion fixture during the Regency!

Plate 6 :

In this third print from *Lady's Monthly Museum* again there are two women — a common theme with this magazine's prints. Here they are walking a dog, who appears to be a poodle, and he (or she) is wearing an ornamental band on its front leg.

Note the high, ruffled collars on both gowns. I am not at all fond of the gown on the right, but I love the huge muff and purple pelerine worn by the lady on the left.

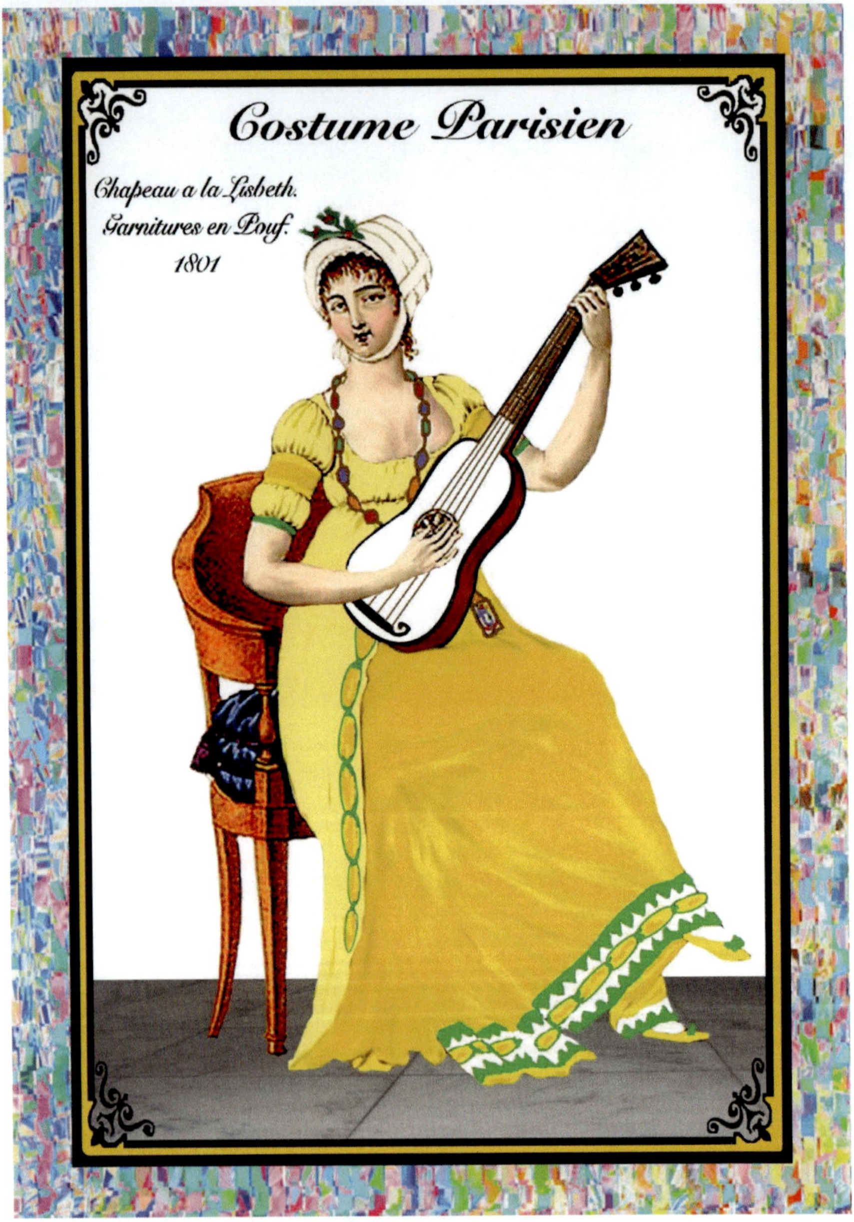

Costume Parisien

Chapeau a la Lisbeth.
Garnitures en Pouf.
1801

Plate 7

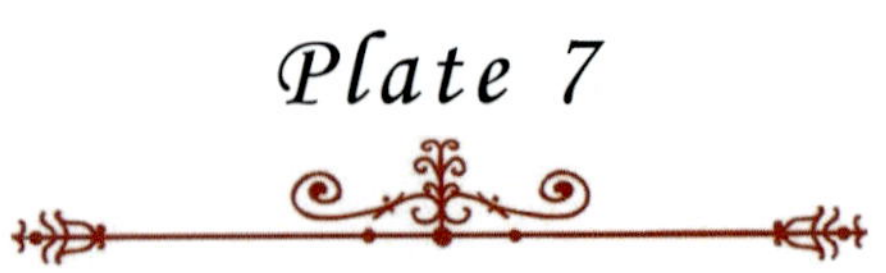

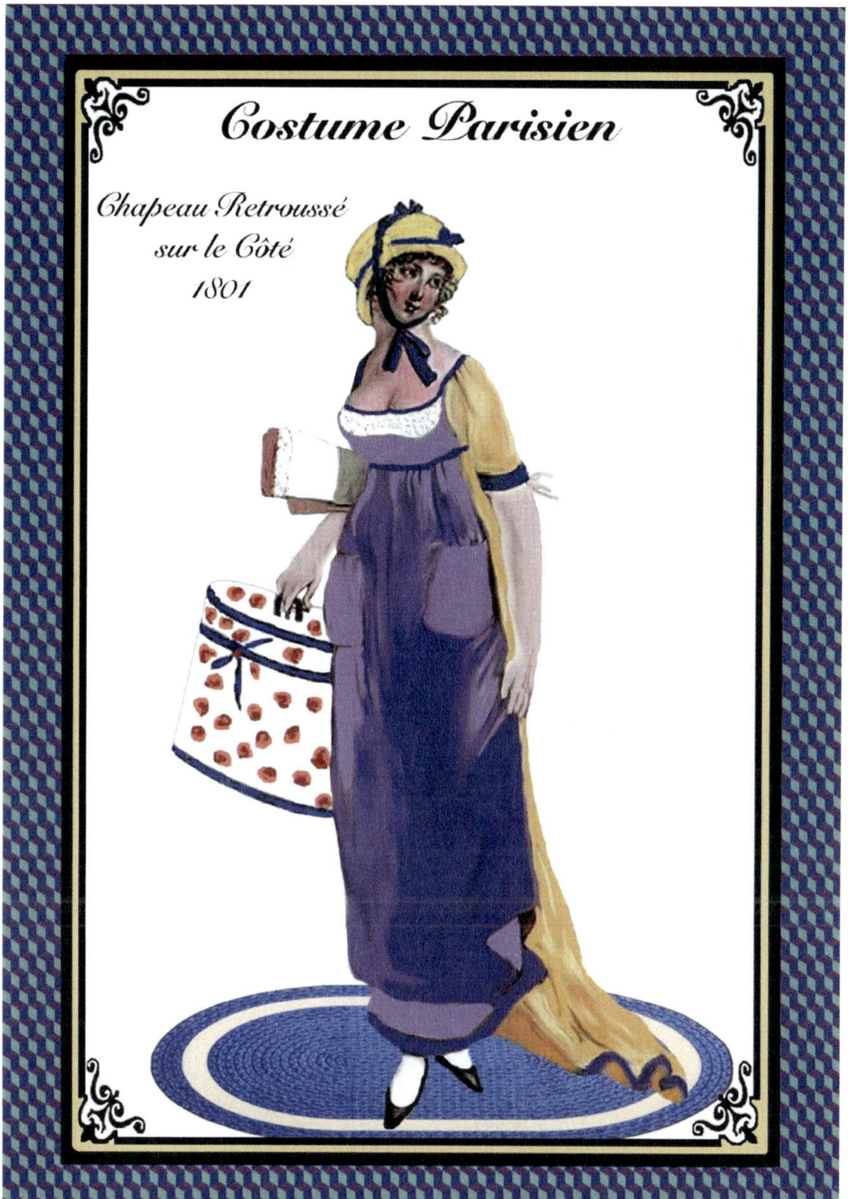

Costume Parisien

Chapeau Retroussé
sur le Côté
1801

Plate 8

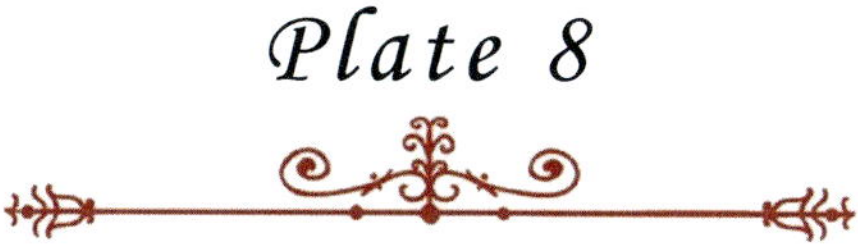

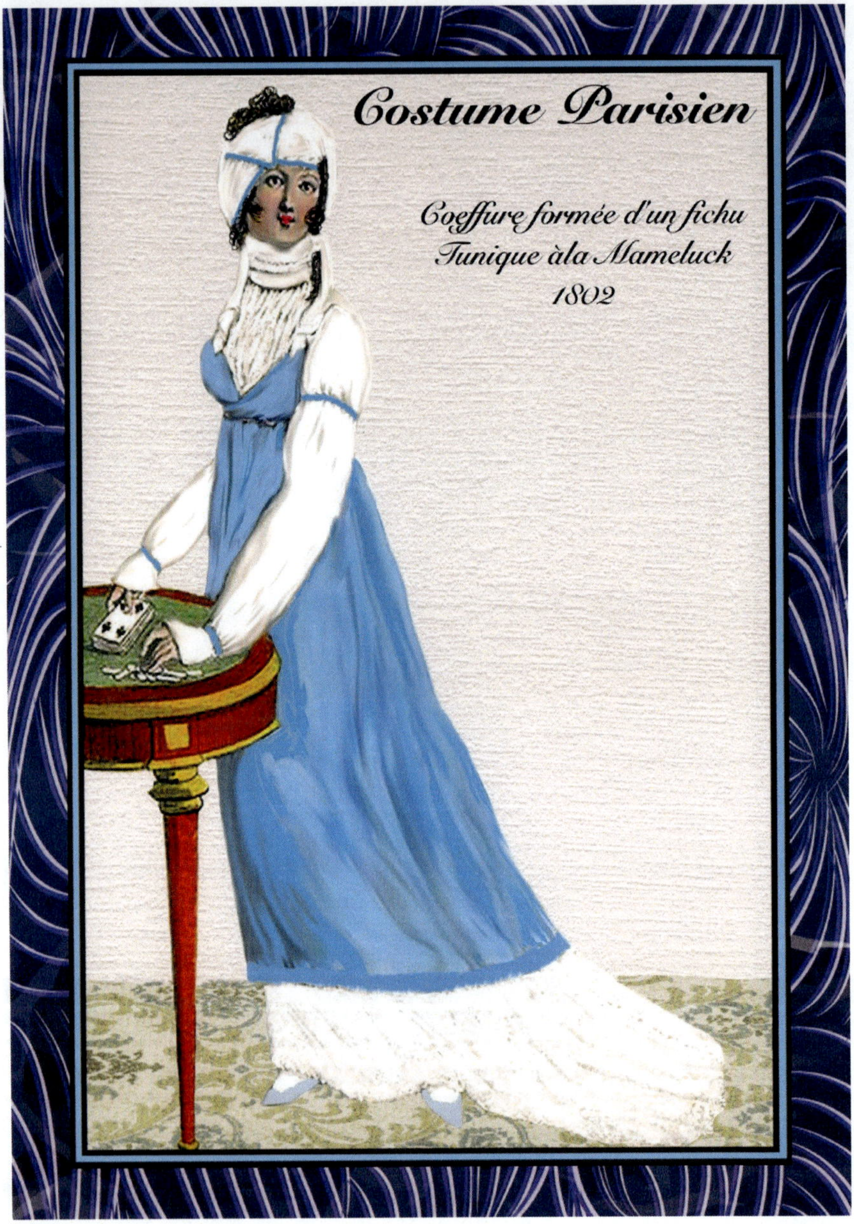

Costume Parisien

Coeffure formée d'un fichu
Tunique àla Mameluck
1802

Plate 9

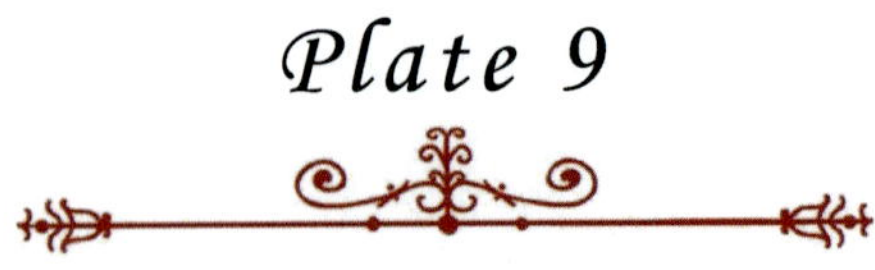

Plate 7 :

Lady playing a guitar. Yes, musical accomplishment was valued and, as seen in this and numerous fashion prints, the pianoforte was not exclusively the instrument of choice! Women learned to play music to entertain guests, but also for personal pleasure.

Translation of the French caption: During the Revolution and Republic periods in France, particular fashion styles were routinely indicated as being "à la" *something*, where the *something* referred to a famous French person (real or fictional) or notable place, event, or object. Lisbeth was a character in a popular play, and as one fashion critic noted: "M. Bertrand flings a large bunch of roses on straw, and it becomes a hat *à la Lisbeth*."

"Garnitures en Pouf" indicates that the hat's trim (*garniture*) is on the outside (*pouf*). Usually "pouf" bonnets were lavishly trimmed, unlike this one.

Plate 8 :

Shopping! When has shopping *not* been a prime diversion for a woman? This lady is wearing a bibbed apron, or pinafore, over her dress, indicating that she may be the shop worker rather than a customer. Under her arm are fabric bolts, and that hat box is huge. Imagine the hat stored inside!

Translation of the French caption: One might presume the *chapeau* in this caption refers to the hat box. However, the translation is, "hat rolls up on the side" so is describing the hat worn by the model.

Plate 9 :

This lady is prepping for serious gaming. She has a deck of cards in hand and a stack of ivory counters ready to go. Card games of various sorts were top entertainments, with gambling for real money common for women as well as men.

Translation of the French caption: Hair styled in ringlets "formed", or contained and shaped, within a fichu. Note how the fichu is carefully wound to hang onto her shoulders and have the edged fabric decoratively triangle on her forehead. Lovely!

A Mameluck (also Mameluk or Mameluce) tunic - *tunique* - was a garment named after an Egyptian military caste, called mamelukes, present during the war with Napoleon. They wore tunics, and with fashion enthralled with everything military, and oriental or exotic, the name stuck.

Costume Parisien
Chapeau de Velours. Plume dite Pleureuse
1802

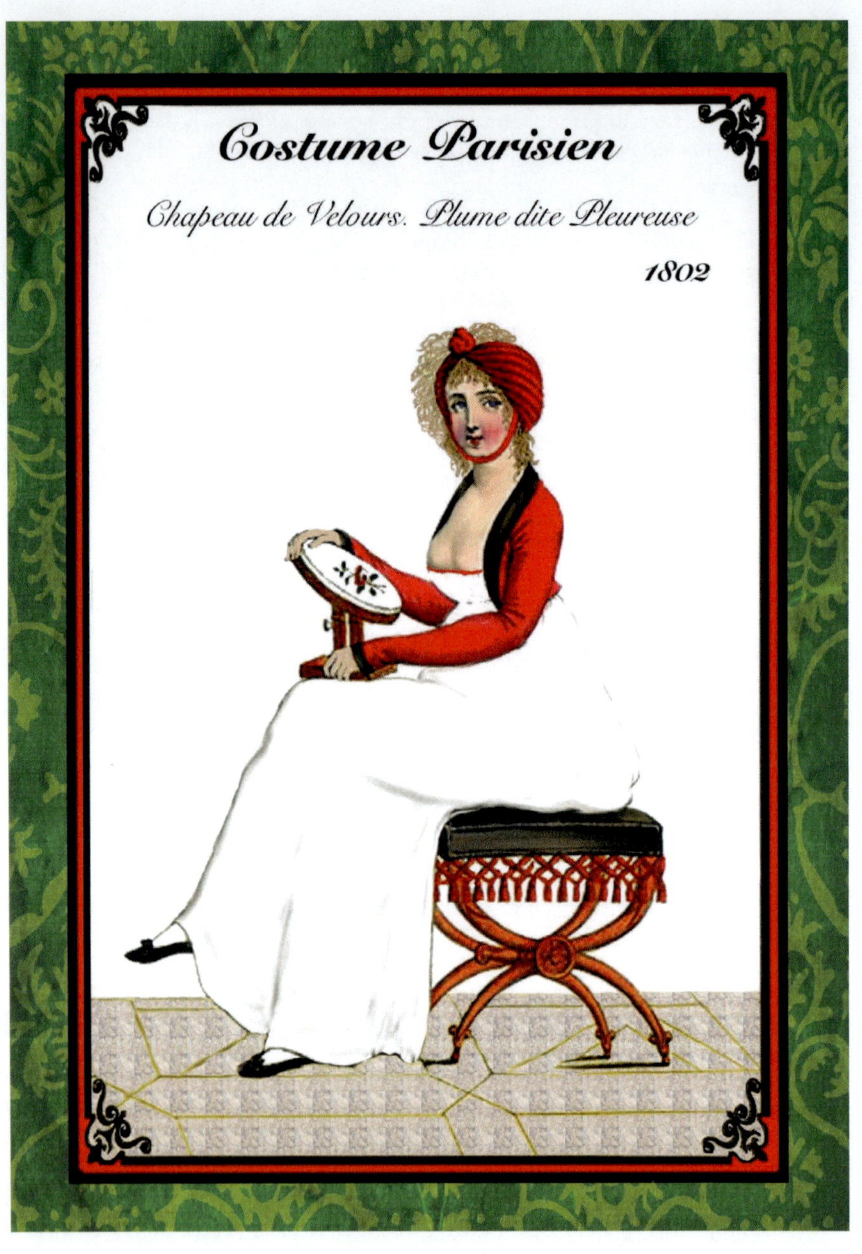

Plate 10

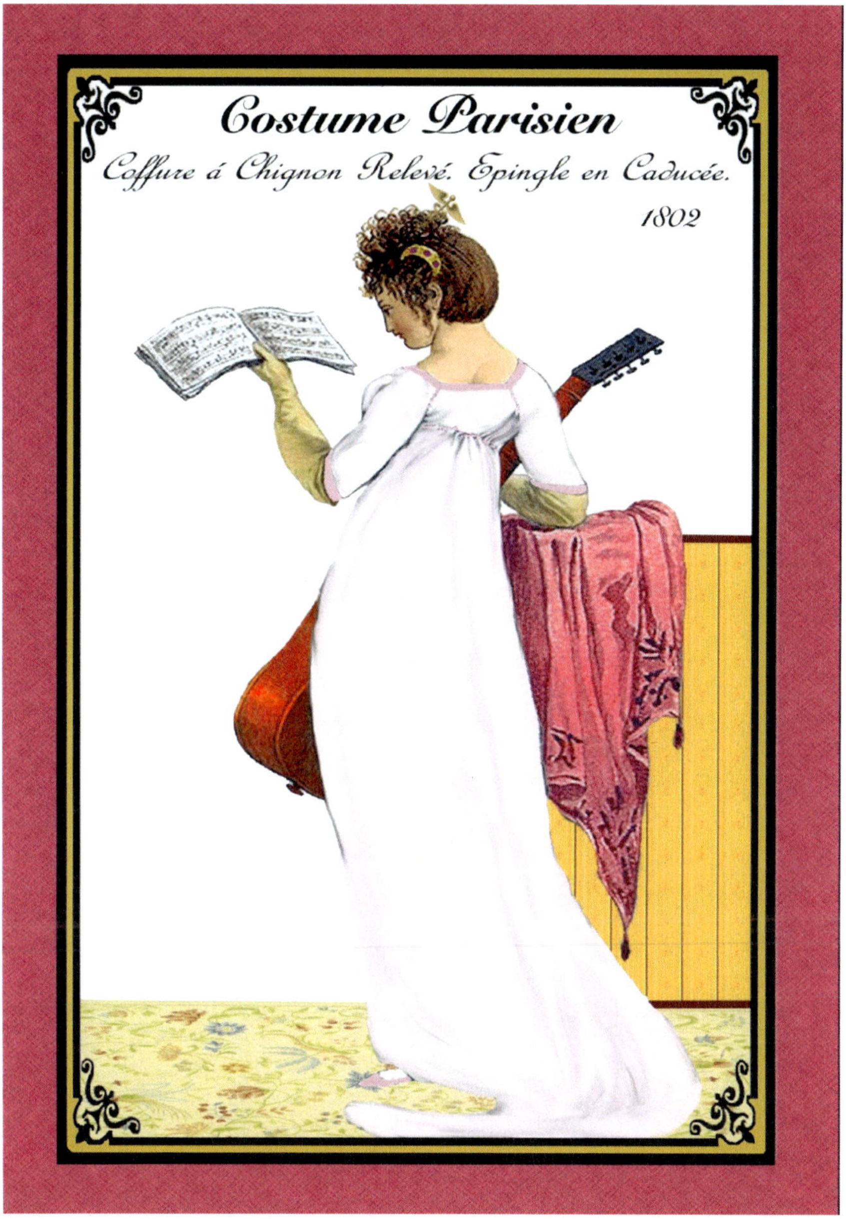

Costume Parisien

Coffure á Chignon Relevé. Epingle en Caducée.

1802

Plate 11

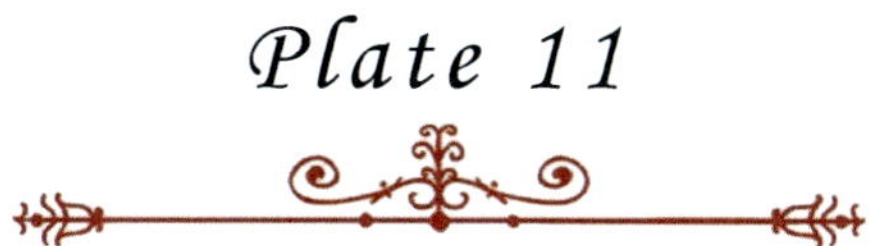

Costume Parisien
Bonnet garni en Tulle.
Fichu sur l' épaule.
1802

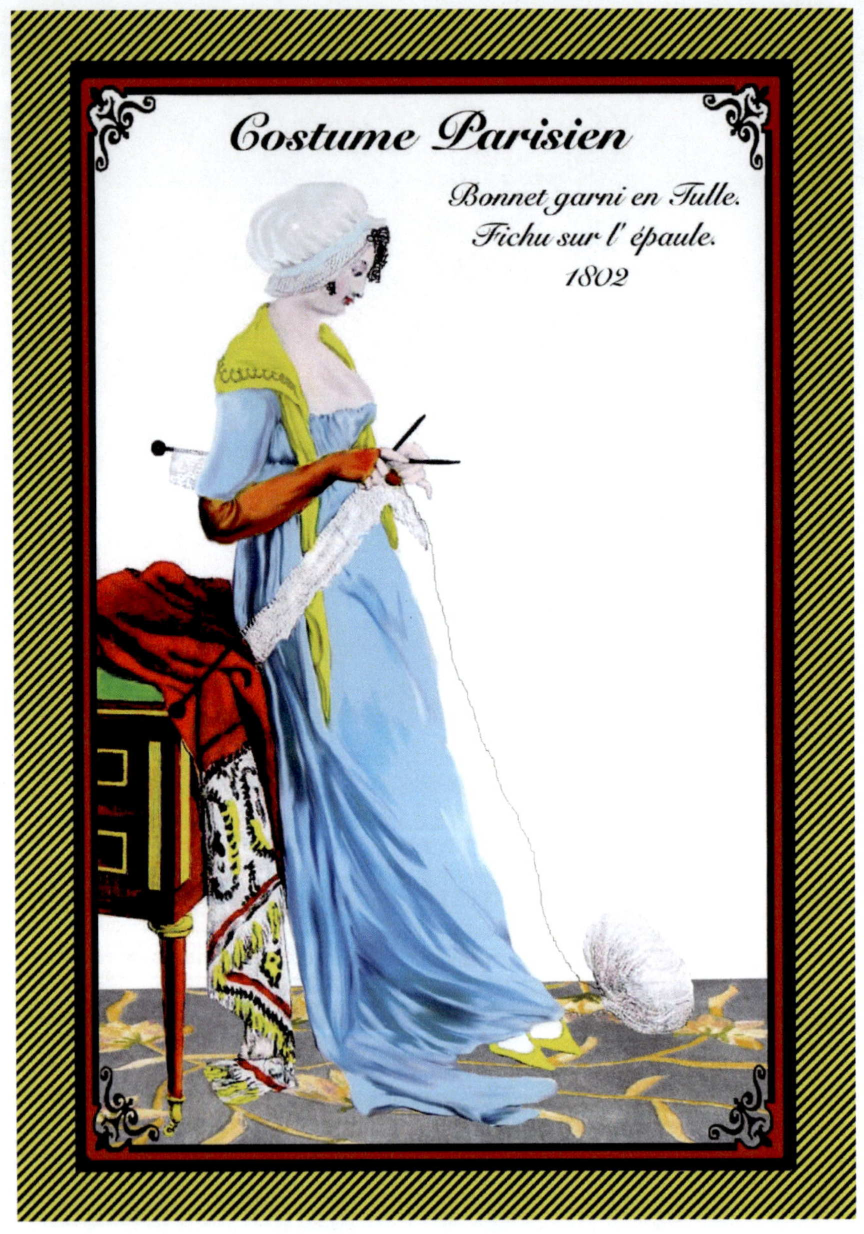

Plate 12

Plate 10 :

A lady embroidering. She uses a tambour frame hoop made of wood attached or resting onto a lap frame allowing both of her hands to be free. Frankly I can't imagine sitting at that angle on a stool, even with the cushion, would be comfortable! The genteel pose works for the fashion print, of course, and that is what matters most.

She wears a very simple gown with a short Spencer jacket not doing an adequate job of covering. Another one of those daring French designs! The caption notes that her hat is made of velour fabric knotted at the crown, and wound so that her curled tresses spill from one side.

Plate 11 :

A lady studying music for the guitar. Compare this guitar to the one held by the lady in Plate #7. Guitars have existed since well before the 12th century and in ages past, as it is still to this day, there have been a plethora of guitar designs. This model is quite large.

Her hairstyle — *Coffure à Chignon* — is gorgeous, and secured with a crescent moon-shaped gold pin. *Epingle en Caducée* is "pin (or hairpin) of Caduceus" and is referring to the *other* hair ornament. Caduceus, the winged staff with two snakes wrapped around it, was the ancient astrological symbol of commerce and is associated with the Greek god Hermes, the messenger for the gods.

Plate 12 :

A lady knitting … while standing up! I know nothing about knitting, but a comment to this fashion plate on Pinterest noted the excessive length of the needles, and that the width of the material indicates a blanket or something similar. Interesting!

Translation of the French caption: "Bonnet trimmed with tulle. Fichu on the shoulders."

Costume Parisien
Coeffure ornée d'une
Fléche et d'un
Peigne renversé
1802

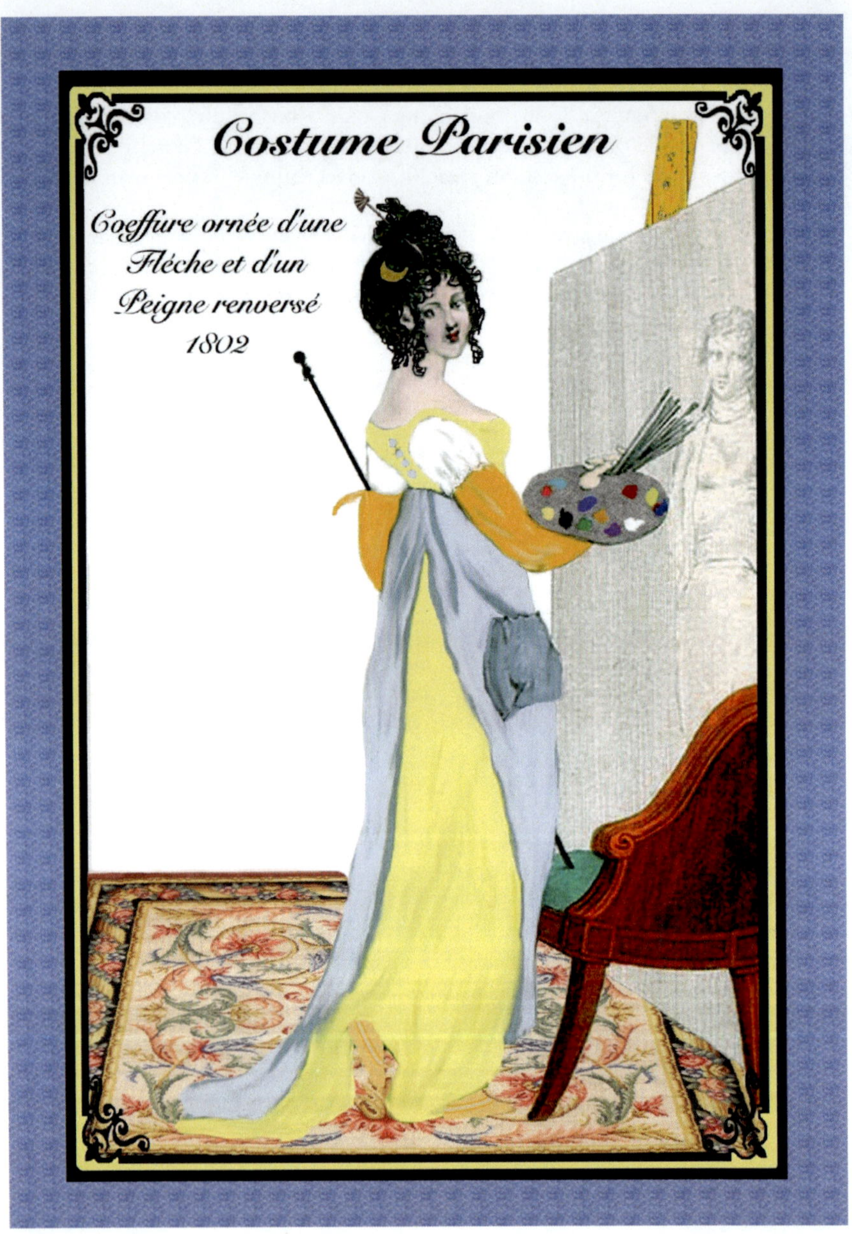

Plate 13

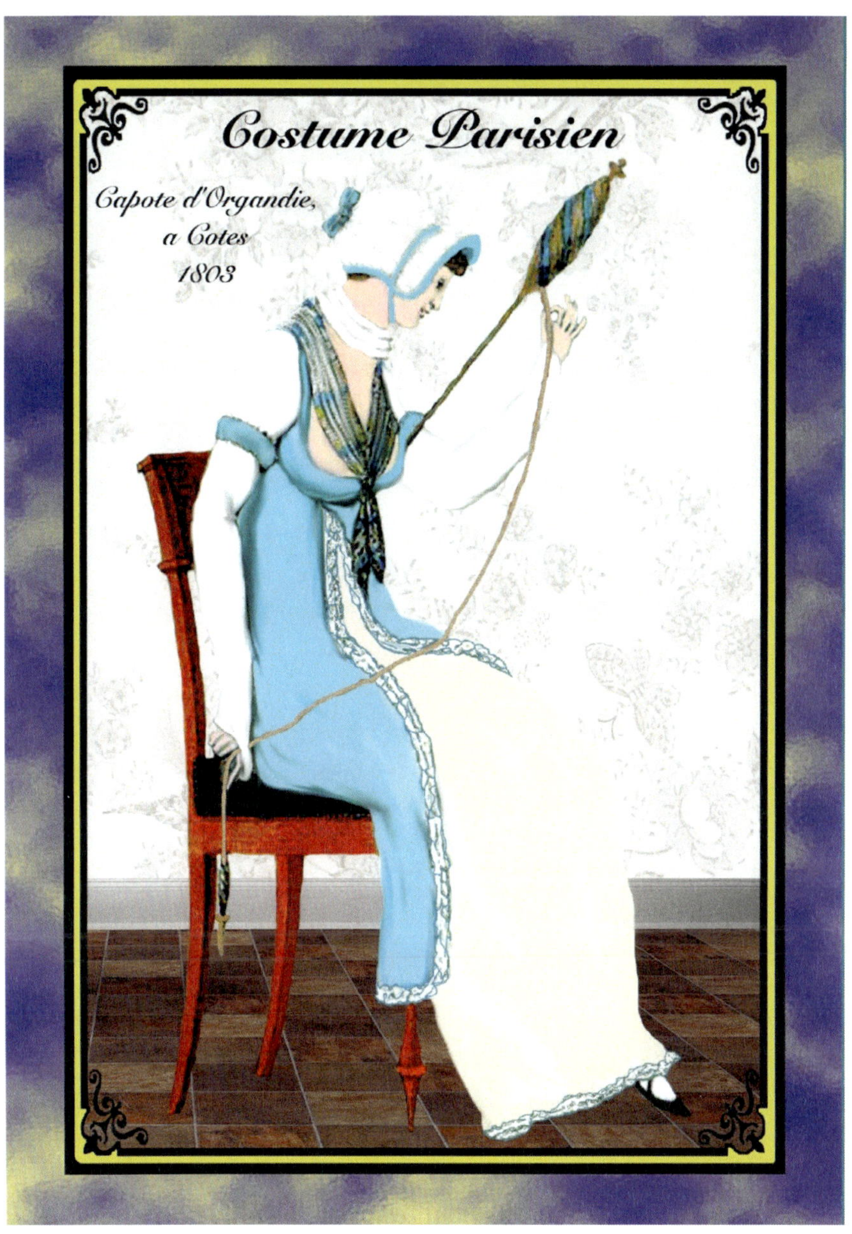

Plate 14

Costume Parisien
Cornette sous un Voile. Garnitures en Fraises
1803

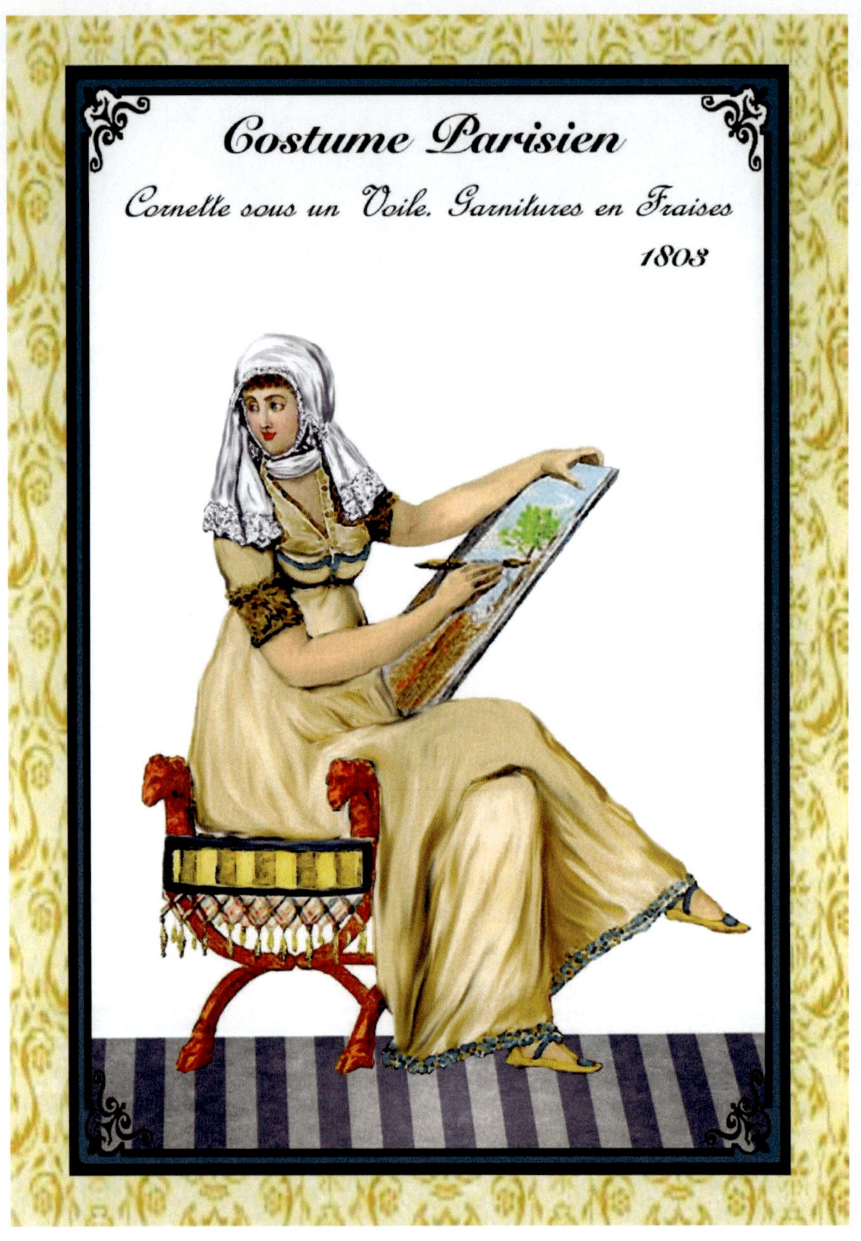

Plate 15

Plate 13 :

A lady painting onto a very large canvas. Who is the gentleman she is painting? Her husband, perhaps? Or a lover? Her gown is protected by an apron, and the long gloves are uniquely designed for messy work. Yet she manages to present a graceful vision of a fashionable lady.

Translation of the French caption: "*Coeffure* adorned with an arrow and a comb reversed." There appears to be a trend in French fashion plates to note the hairstyle, ornaments, and type of hat more often than the garments. In this case, I can understand why! Her hair is fabulously coiffed and adorned.

Plate 14 :

This lady is spinning yarn by hand. She is using a drop spindle (the dangling portion) with a weighted whorl that twists the loose fiber wound around the distaff tucked under her arm.

Translation of the French caption: "Hood of organza…with sides." The hood here is the hat, which has sides (or a wide brim), and is made of organza. Organza (or organdy) is a thin, transparent fabric made from silk or muslin with a stiff, crisp finish. Very durable, and perfect for covering or trimming a hat.

Plate 15 :

Lady painting an outdoor scenic picture.

Translation of the French caption: *Cornette*, or Cornet, *sous un Voile* (under the veil) was a style of covering the hair completely, as commonly worn for sleeping or by women in certain religious orders. Hence the phrase, "taking the veil." Whether this print is implying she is of a religious order is unclear, but doubtful considering the gown and slippers she is wearing.

Garnitures en fraises, literally "trimmed in strawberries," was a pleating method that created puckers resembling the seeds on strawberries. This technique is seen here framing her face and along the dangling edges of the *cornette*.

This stool is a popular period design with the supports carved into animal head shapes, and the animal's paws carved into a monopodia (single-base) style inspired by ancient Greek, Roman, and Egyptian designs.

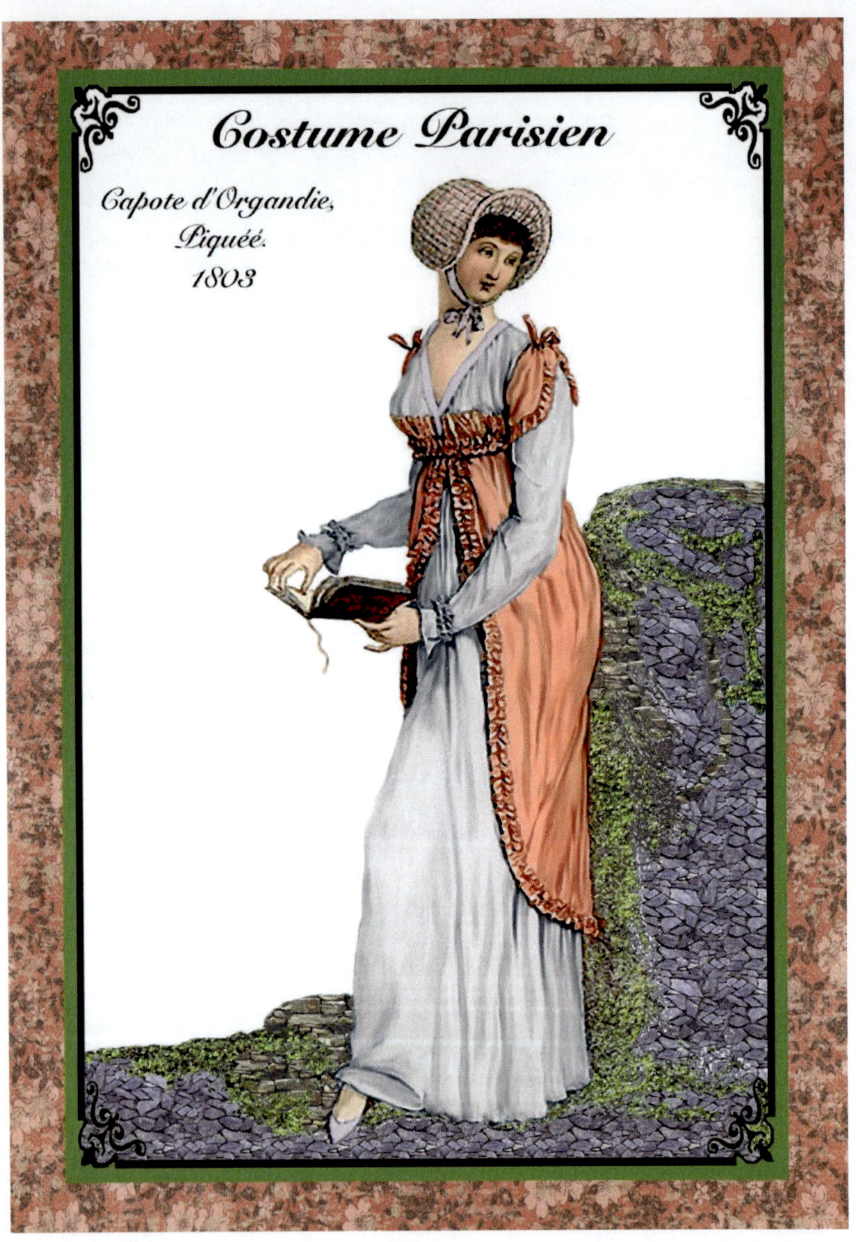

Plate 16

Costume Parisien
Turban à la Mameluck.
Boucles d'Oreilles de Corail.
1803

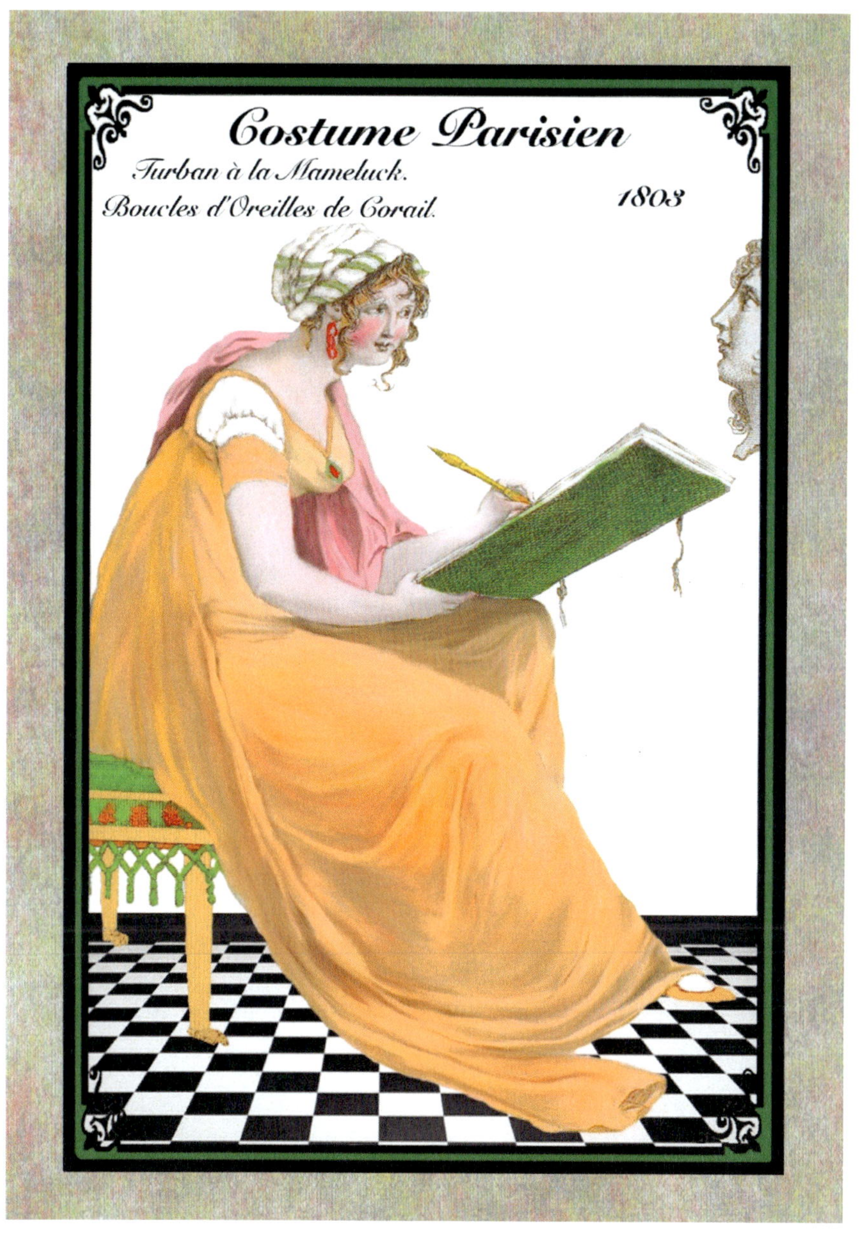

Plate 17

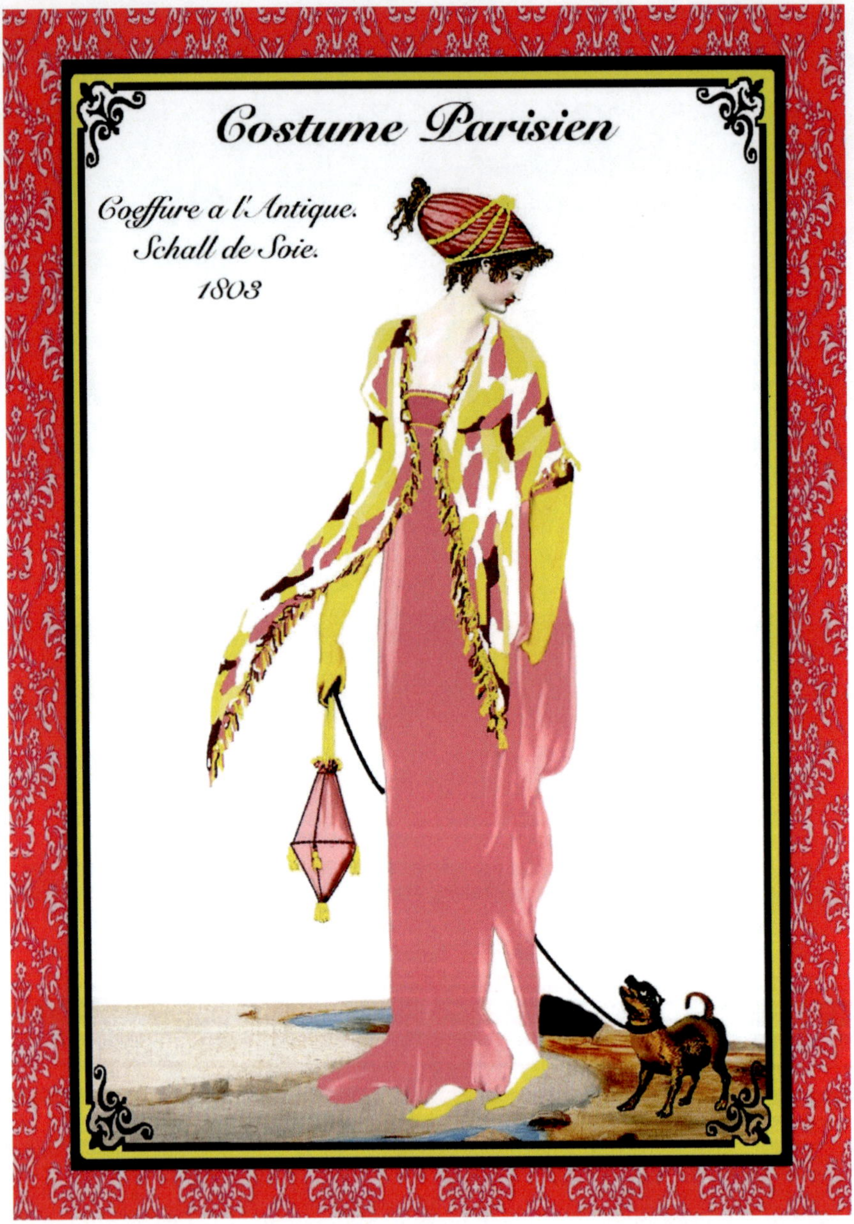

Costume Parisien

Coeffure a l'Antique.
Schall de Soie.
1803

Plate 18

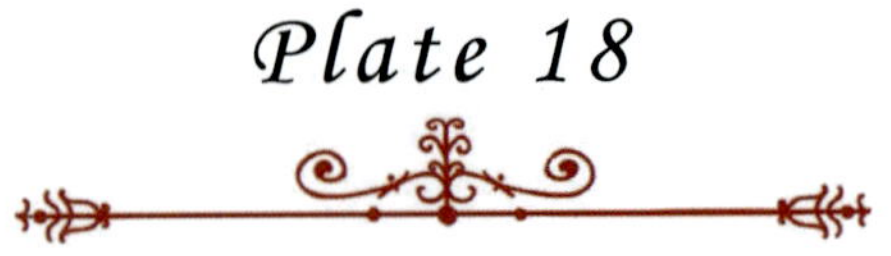

Plate 16 :

A lady improving her mind by reading while maintaining her health and vigor by walking outdoors. This could be Elizabeth Bennet!

Translation of the French caption: As noted in Plate #14, *Capote d'Organdie* refers to the brimmed, stiff hat covered and/or trimmed with organza. *Piquéé* is a French word with dozens of meanings, although in this case my guess is this translation from the Centre National de Resources Textuelles et Lexicales: "a fabric, a garment or garment part, which is formed of two superimposed fabric layers, held in place by stitches forming a regular pattern; and, thick fabric fashioned, usually cotton, the weaving forming geometric designs similar to pitting." The bibbed apron fits that description.

Plate 17 :

Once again a lady passing her time in an artistic pursuit.

Translation of the French caption: *Turban à la Mameluck*. As noted previously, the French were obsessed with bestowing popular names onto garments, in this print the turban given the *Mameluck* moniker! See Plate #9 about the mameluck. *Boucles d'Oreilles de Corail* is literally "rings of variable shapes and sizes, on the external ear (earlobe), made of coral."

Plate 18 :

How cute is that puppy! Animals as pets, especially tiny dogs, date back to the dawn of time, I suspect. And with a pet comes responsibility, such as taking him for a walk. Plus, imagine how perfect an adorable pooch is as a conversation starter. If a gentleman is wise he will know that expressing delight over a lady's pet is a sure way to win her affections!

Translation of the French caption: *Antique* today refers to anything older than a hundred years or so. For the French Empire and English Regency people, *antique* meant the Greco-Roman era of classical antiquity.

Schall de Soie means "shawl of silk," a rather blah caption for this stunning print. And I have to say I want that reticule, tassels and all!

Costume Parisien
Amazone en Robe de Linon.
Spencer de-drap,
Chapeau Jockei.
1798

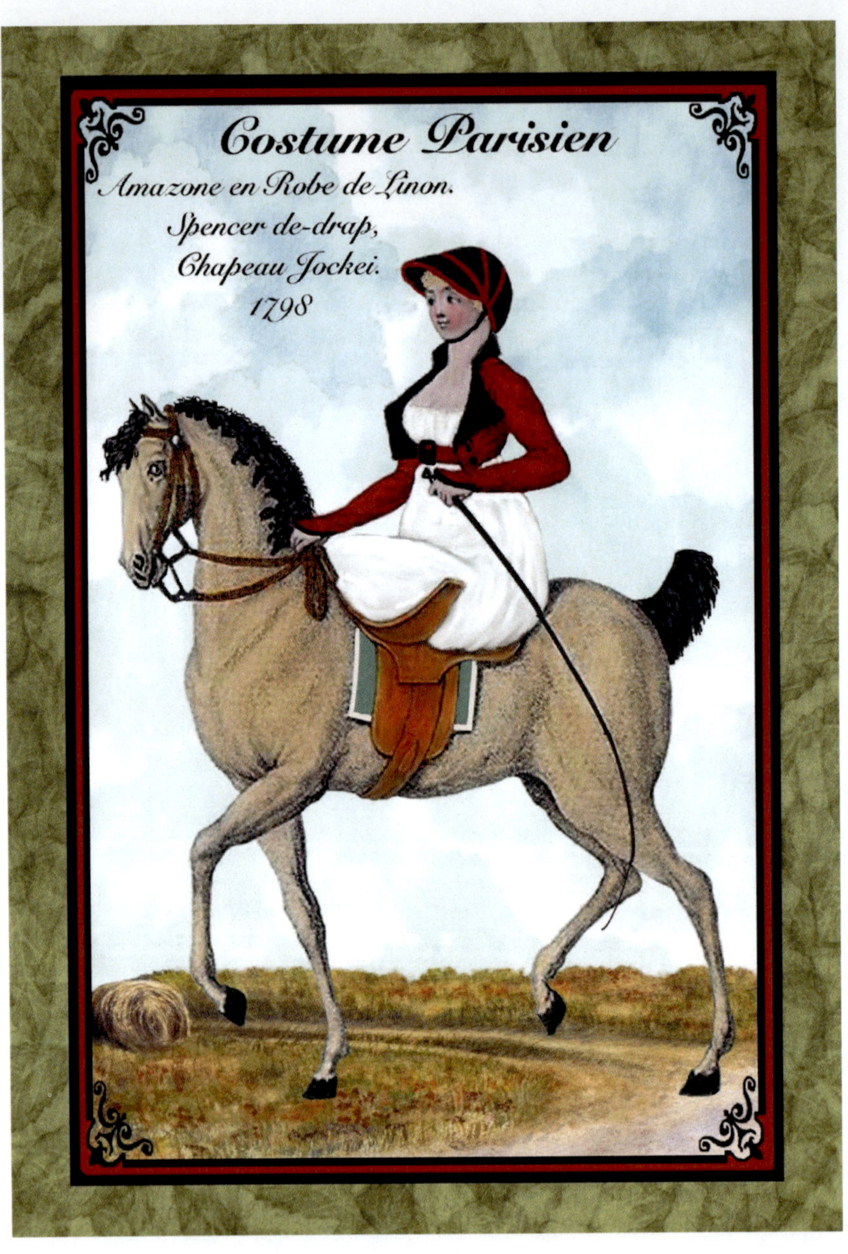

Plate 19

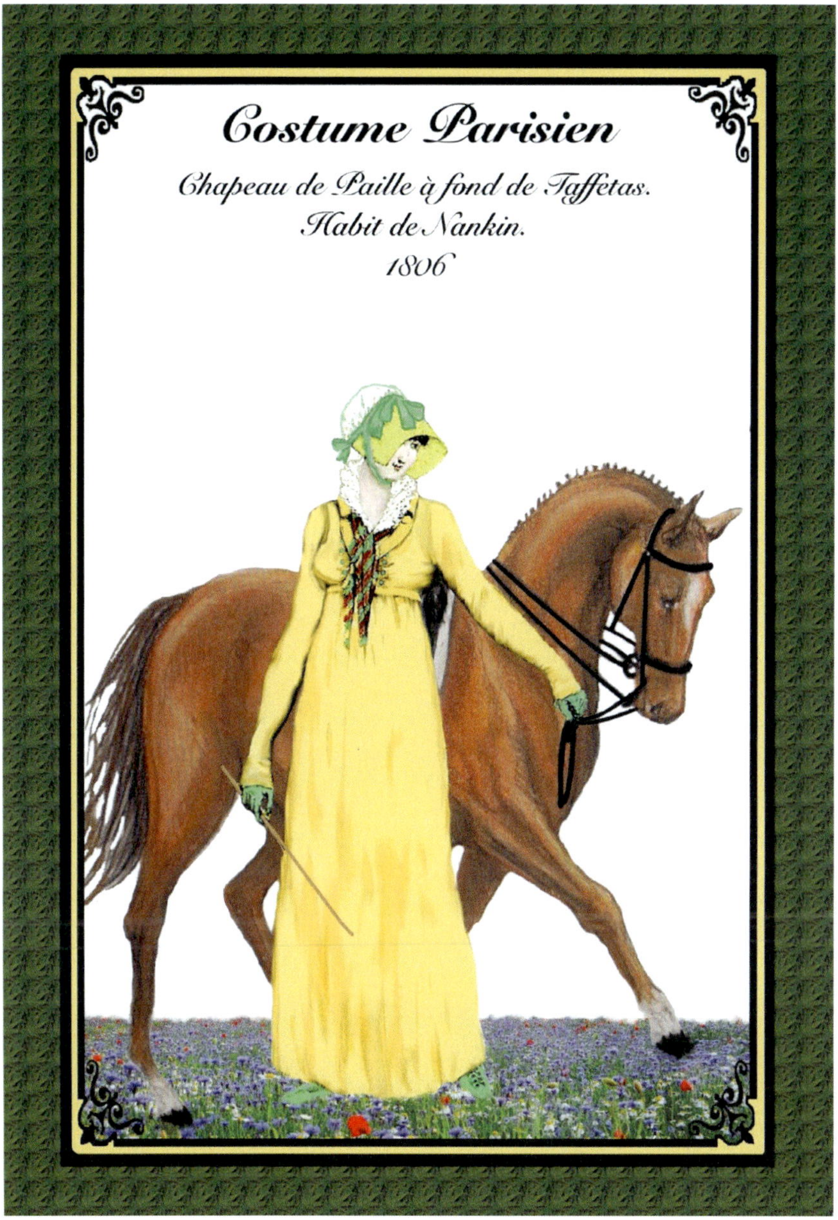

Costume Parisien

Chapeau de Paille à fond de Taffetas.
Habit de Nankin.
1806

Plate 20

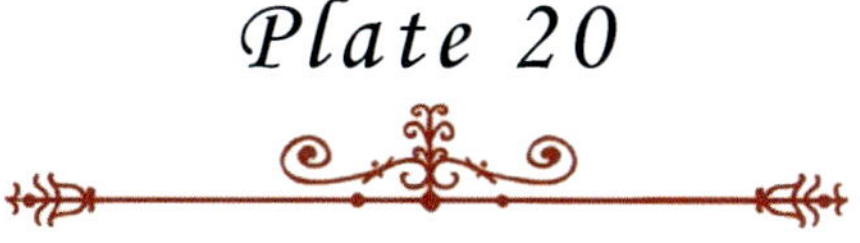

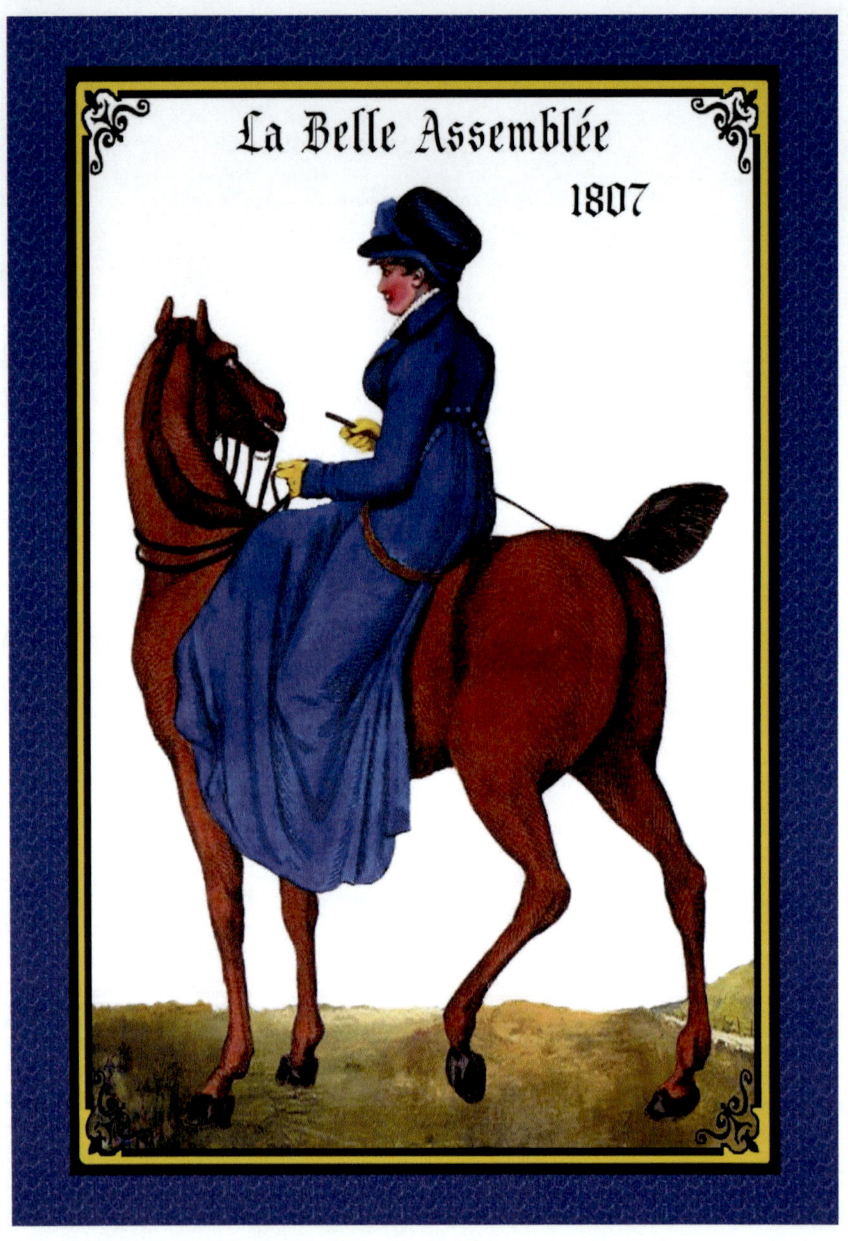

Plate 21

Plate 19 :

First in a print trio of ladies and horses, this one from 1798 shows a lady riding sidesaddle (as they all did, if being proper). This is a particularly excellent drawing capturing the construction of a woman's saddle. Riding jackets and habits were primarily sewn and designed by male tailors until the second decade of the 19th century, and thus were typically of a more masculine structure.

The word *Amazone* — "Woman soul of manly allure" — became the standard term for a woman's riding habit. In this print her riding garment is described as a dress (*robe*) of linen, with a Spencer jacket in a resistant wool fabric whose fibers are felted (*de-drap*) so probably broadcloth, and a jockey-style cap. Note the tight fit of the jacket and the buckled belt around her waist, which may well be a part of the jacket, designed to support the bosom and protect the chest. When actually riding the horse, the Spencer would be buttoned securely.

Plate 20 :

In this 1806 fashion plate we can see the riding habit's formed fit to the torso, and the voluminous skirt. Riding habits were full and gathered in the back, usually with a train, to ensure the legs were covered when in the sidesaddle to maintain modesty.

Nankin, as the caption indicates this outfit is made of, was a canvas cotton fabric woven tight and solid, light yellow, originally manufactured in Nanjing, and mainly used in the menswear (breeches, especially) due to the durability. Perfect for horse riding. *Paille* is a type of straw woven into hats (in this case the brim) with the cap, or "back" portion (*à fond*) made of taffeta.

Plate 21 :

Caption on this plate: "A French lady, mounted on horseback in the most fashionable style, for the *Long Champs* and *Elysées*, at Paris."

Description from the March 1807 edition of *La Belle Assemblée*: "An equestrian habit of fine seal-wool cloth, with elastic strap; the colour blue (but olive, or puce, are equally esteemed), with convex buttons of dead gold. The habit to sit high in the neck behind, lapelled in front, and buttoned twice at the small of the waist; a high plaited frill of cambric, uniting at the bosom where the habit closes. A jockey bonnet of the same materials as composes the habit, finished with a band and tuft in front. Hair in dishevelled crop. York tan gloves; and demi-boots of purple kid, laced with jonquille chord."

Sadly the boots are not seen, which seems odd to me after being described!

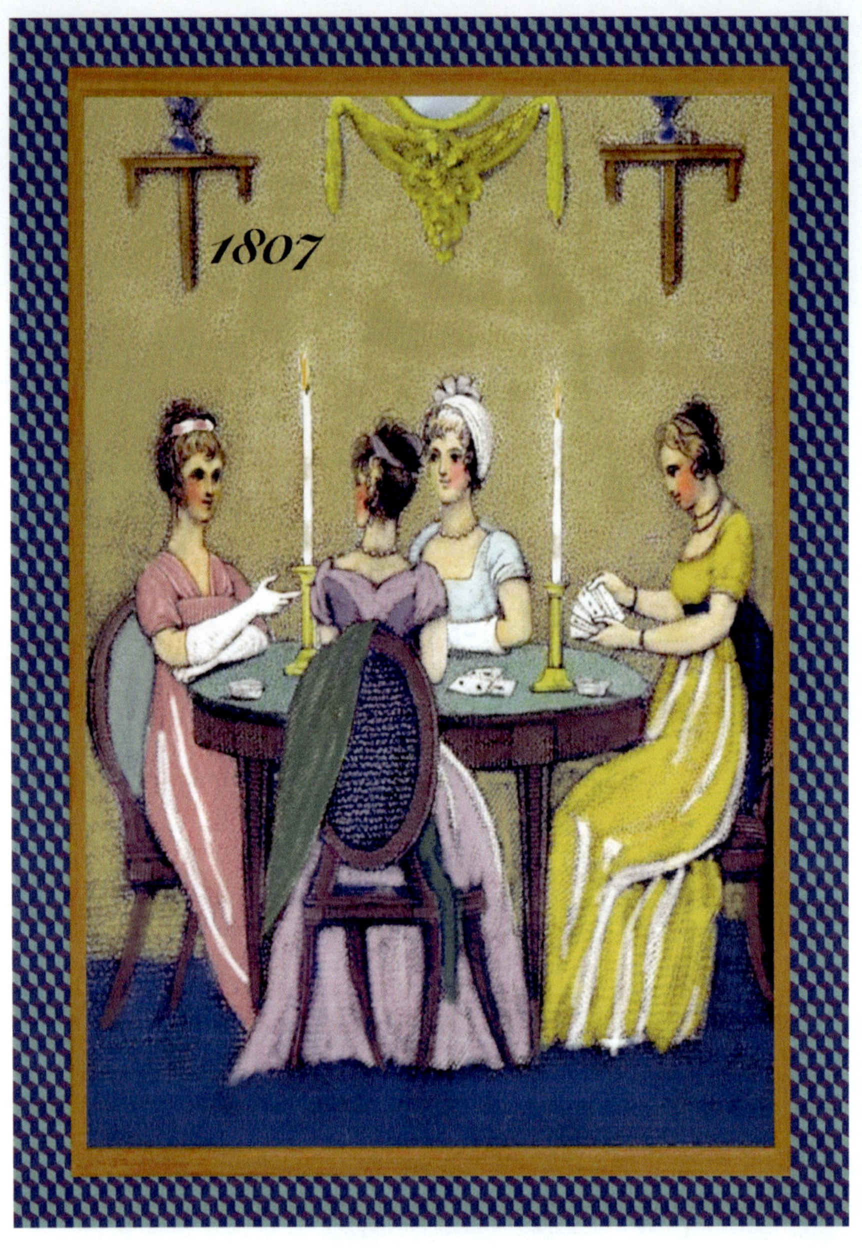

Plate 22

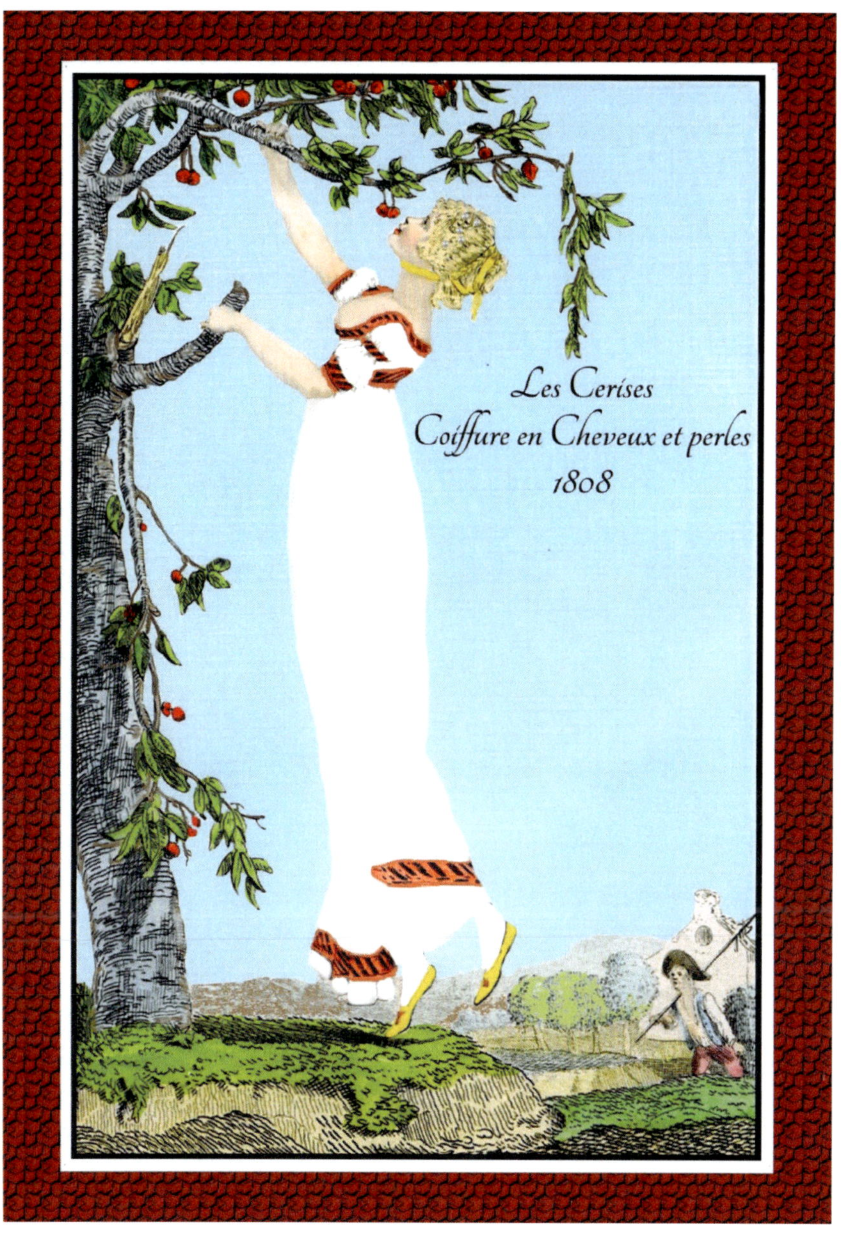

Plate 23

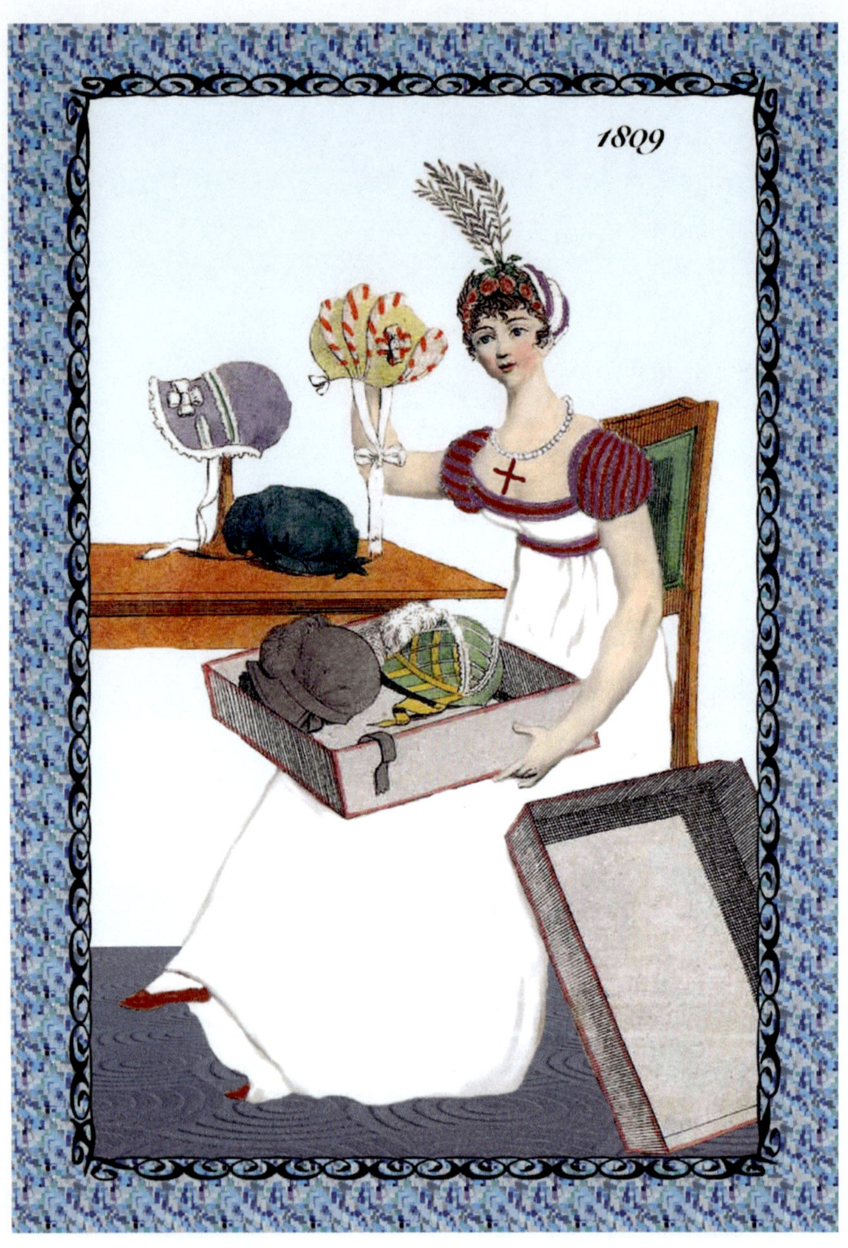

Plate 24

Plate 22 :

Card parties were a popular evening entertainment. Loo, whist, piquet, quadrille, faro ... the variety of games played in the Regency were numerous. Gambling, for low or high stakes, enhanced the challenge. In this print two small bowls sitting on the table would have been used to hold each lady's counters, an indication that score was being kept and monetary betting going on.

The original is marked as, "Print designed and engraved by F. Eginton of Birmingham." and was published in the 1807 edition of *The New Bath Guide* by Christopher Anstey (1724-1805). *The New Bath Guide* is a collection of Anstey's poems and personal observations of Bath in England. The poem accompanying this image is another strong indication of money at stake.

They toil not indeed, nor indeed do they spin.
Yet they never are idle when once they begin.
But are very intent on increasing their store.
And always keep shuffling & cutting for more.

Plate 23 :

Les Cerises, or The Cherries. This print is one of my favorites. A beautiful dress worn by a pretty blonde (an unusual hair color in French fashion plates) who appears to have walked onto the tenant farmer's field to feast on fresh cherries. The tiptoe pose, brilliant colors, and background landscape are fantastic.

Printed in *Modes et Manières du Jour* — Methods and Ways of the Day — the French caption describes her hair as *cheveux*, meaning "natural color" and/or "undone, tousled," that is adorned with pearls.

Plate 24 :

Oh, so many hats and only one head! What is a lady to do? Staying abreast of the latest fashions, and the pursuit of new accoutrements, required a fair amount of time. And, in light of the vast quantity of magazine fashion plates, it was a passionate entertainment.

This print shows six different hat styles, in a variety of colors.

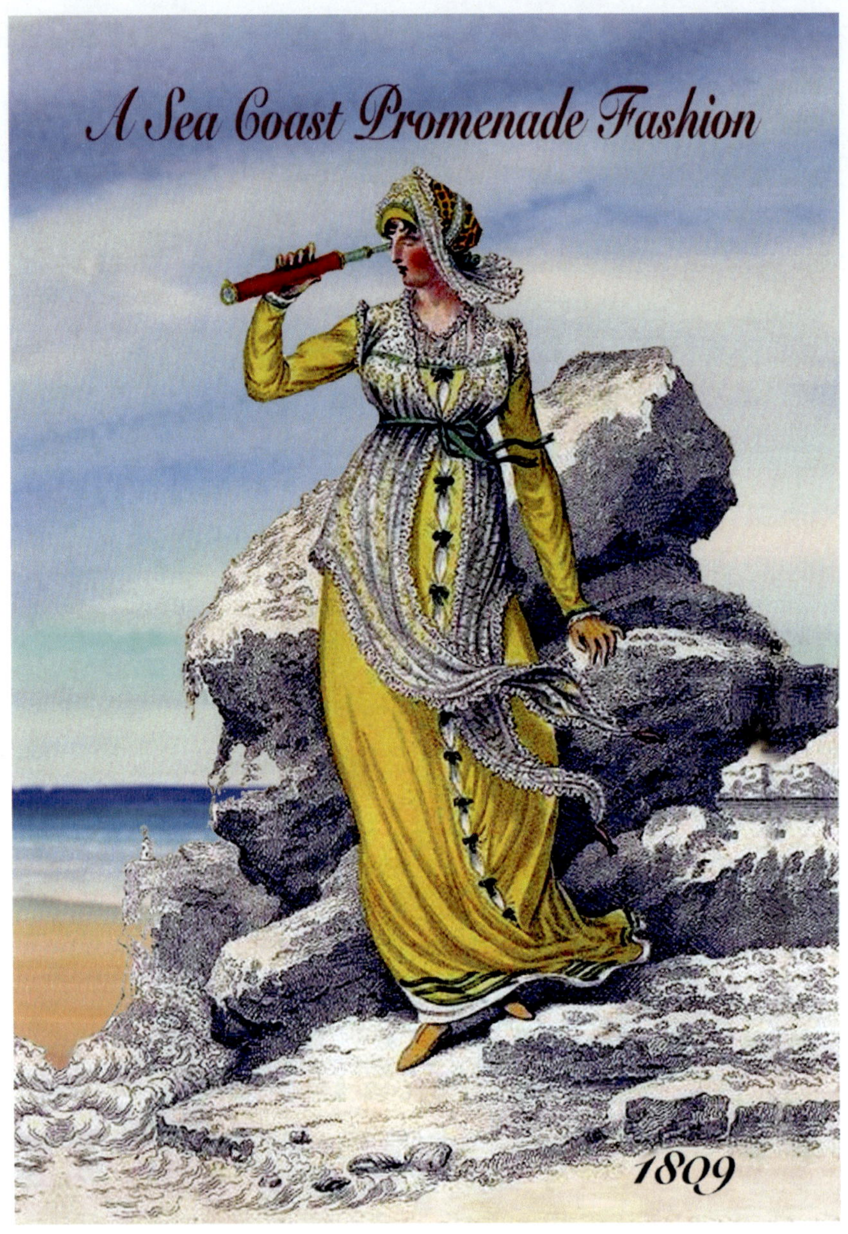

Plate 25

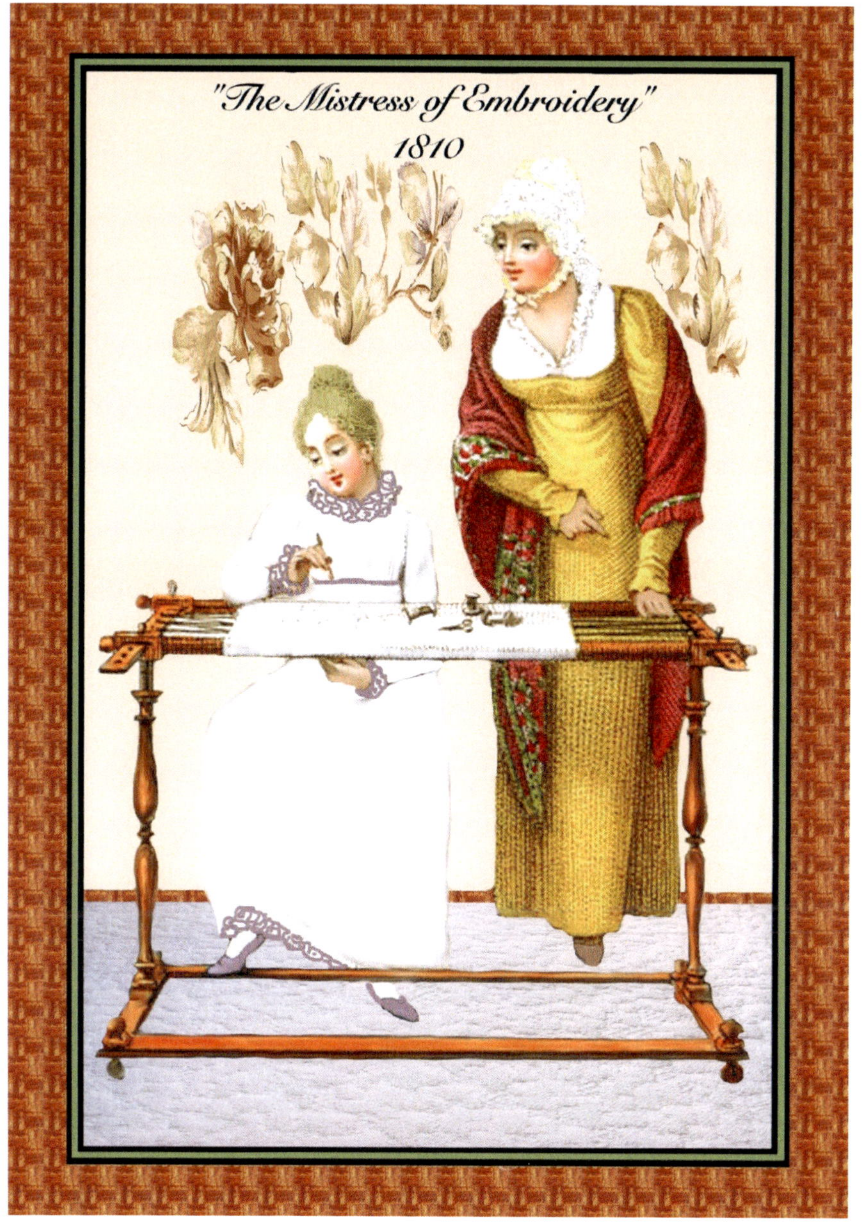

Plate 26

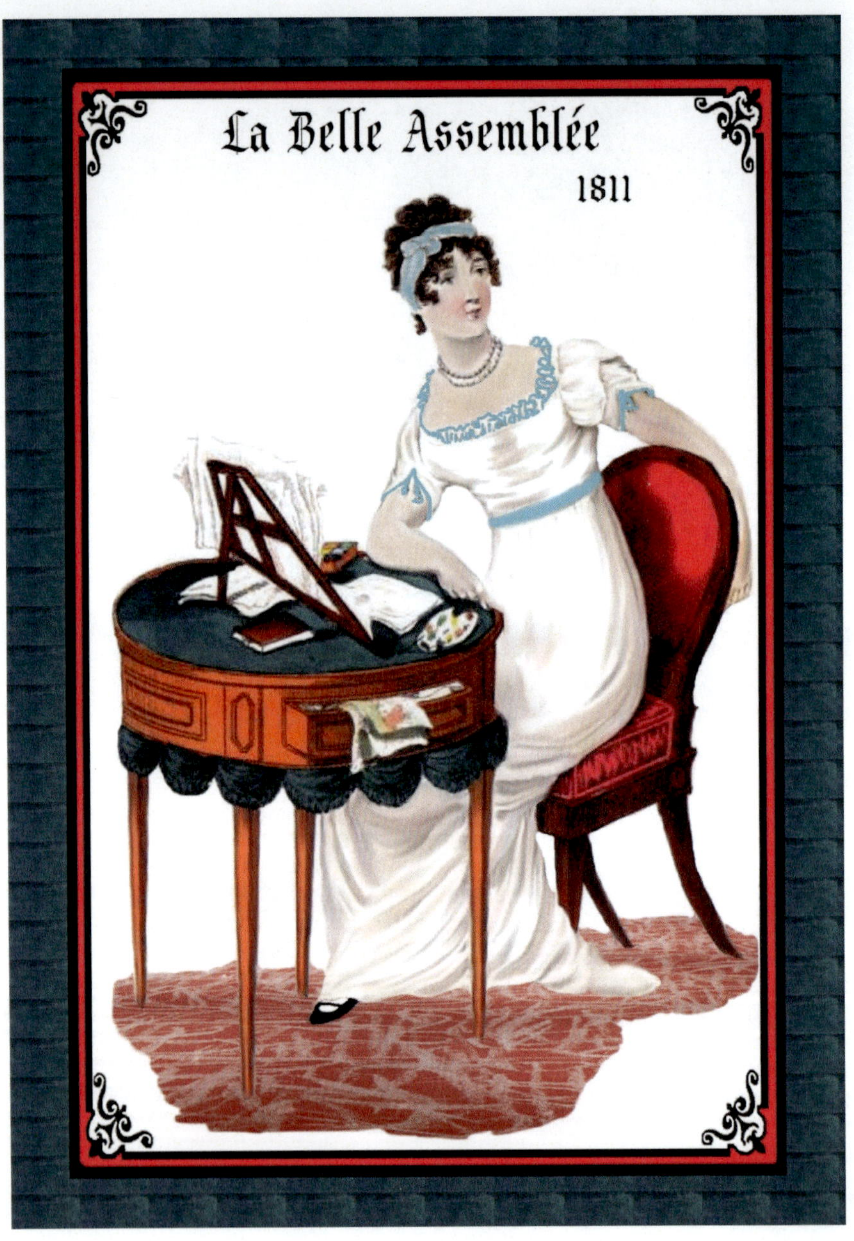

Plate 27

Plate 25 :

Holidays at the seaside were so popular that entire fashions evolved. This print is from the October 1809 edition of *La Belle Assemblée.*

The description in the magazine is as follows: "A dress worn by a lady at Brighton. A bonnet of yellow satin and lace, richly embossed with leopard spots in deep orange; the front in the tiara form, bound with green ribband; a band of the same confines the crown, and ties in a bow behind; a robe of yellow craped muslin made to sit tight to the figure confined at the bosom and down the front with knots of green ribband, round the neck and ornamented round the bottom with three rows of the same; sleeves with small lace ruffles hemmed to correspond; a lace tucker, fastened on the bosom with an Egyptian pebble. A zephyr cloak of rich lace falling in long points to the feet, finished with silk tassels, sloped up in the form of a jacket behind, meeting at the bosom and on the shoulders, confined with graceful negligence to the form by a sash of green ribband. Yellow Morocco sandals; gloves of York tan."

Plate 26 :

These ladies are using a free-standing embroidery frame necessary for large needlework projects, as well as other forms of canvas work, in order to keep the entire piece of fabric taut. Constructed of wood with two rollers for the top and base, and two side pieces. A piece of fabric was securely nailed or stapled along each of the rollers, and holes in the frame's ends held the side pieces secured in place with wing nuts to adjust the width of the frame and the tautness of the stretched fabric.

This print by artist Augustin Legrand (1765-1815) was the front piece of *The Mistress of Embroidery: A Small Treatise on the Art of Embroidering,* a book published in 1816 by an "English lady."

Plate 27 :

This style of round table with drawers all around the platform was known as a "drum table." The drawers were often divided into smaller compartments for organization.

The description in the magazine is as follows: "A white cambric frock, with a demi train; short sleeves fastened up in front with cordon and tassels; a necklace formed of two rows of opal; the hair dressed in full curls, and confined by a demi-turban of very fine muslin tied on the right side with a small bow; silk stockings with lace clocks, richly brocaded, and plain black kid slippers."

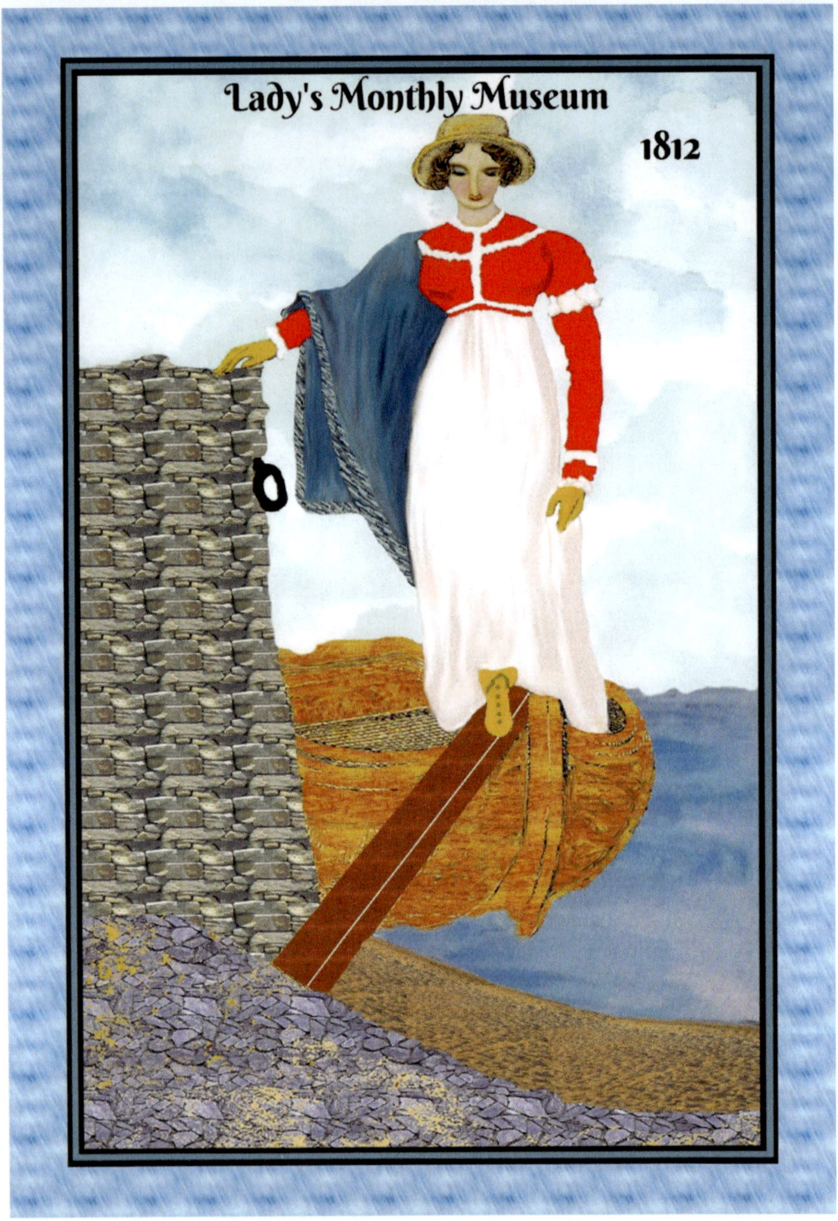

Lady's Monthly Museum

1812

Plate 28

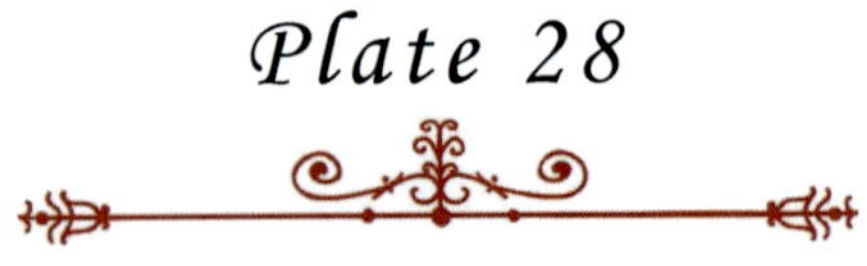

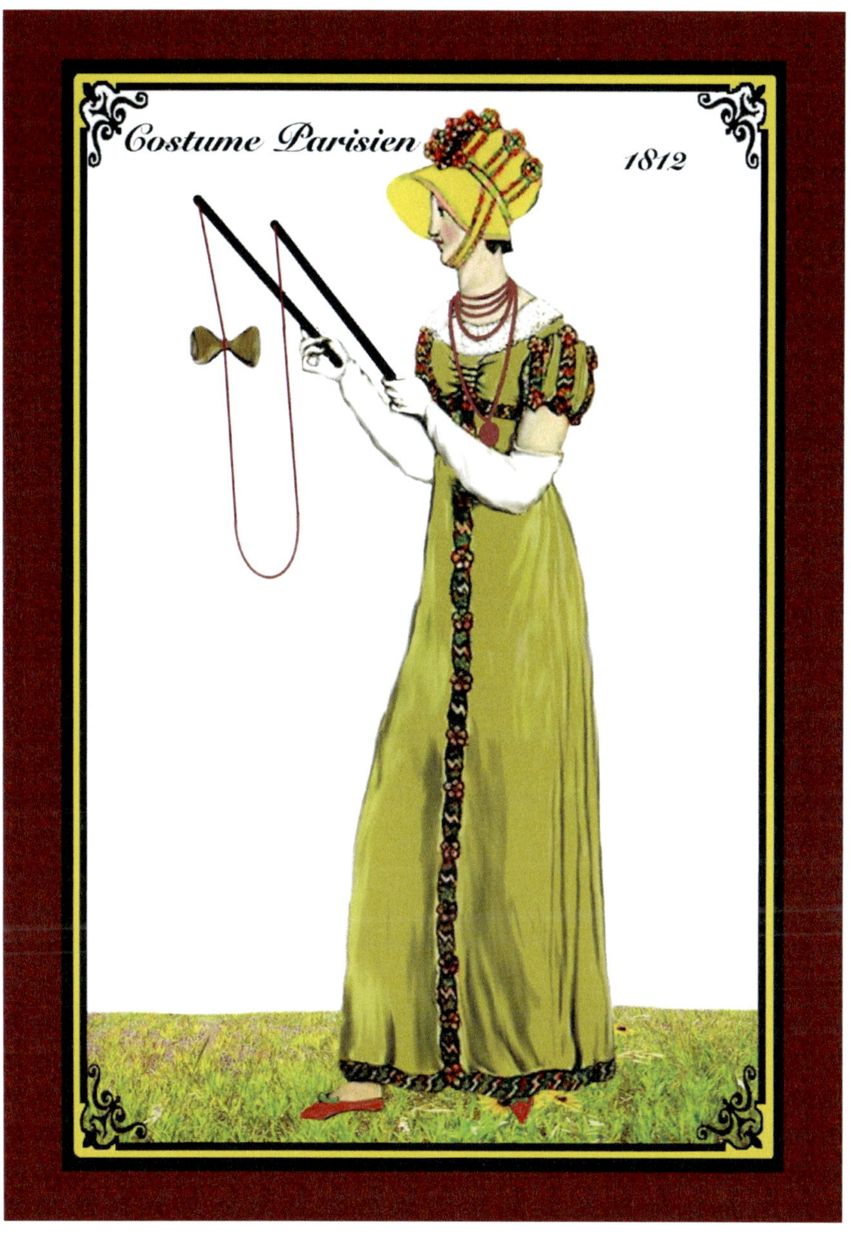

Plate 29

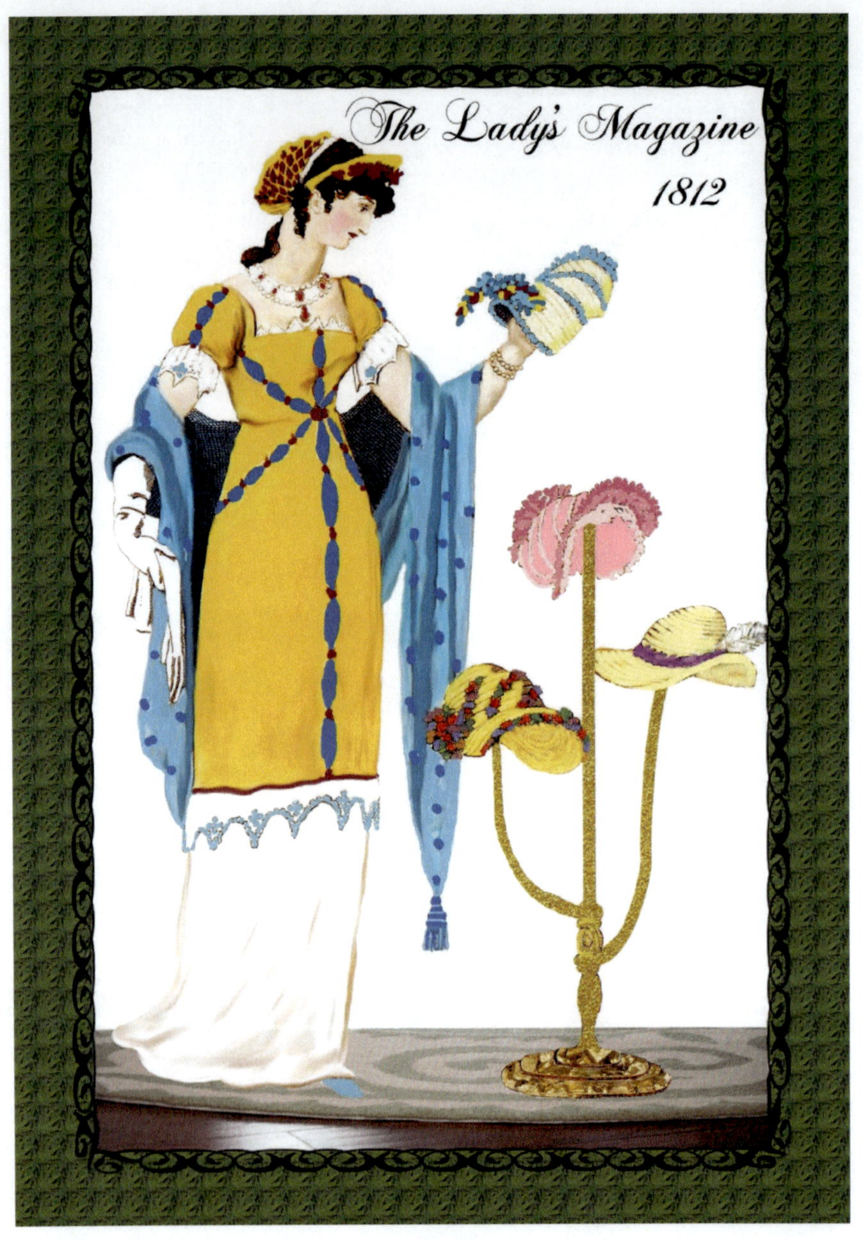

Plate 30

Plate 28 :

The fisherwoman in me was instantly drawn to this print. The original has the lady all in white with the shawl a dull blue, and the scenery (including the boat) simple line drawings devoid of color or detail. I had so much fun adding the graphics and bright colors!

From the October issue description: "Morning Dress. A white mull muslin dress trimmed with lace, sleeves full at top, and ruffle of lace round the wrist; shawl of Salamanca blue; chip hat; boots and gloves of yellow kid, or jean."

The commentary leads me to speculate whether the artist drew a boat for uniqueness — A morning dress for rowing in a small boat? Nevertheless, ladies did sail and row boats, and even fished.

Plate 29 :

Young lady playing with a *diabolo*. Evolved from the Chinese yo-yo, the *diabolo* is a juggling prop consisting of an axle and two cups or round discs. It is unknown precisely who invented the *diabolo*, but French and English missionaries are credited with bringing the game to Europe centuries ago. By the end of the 18th century the game, known as "devil on two sticks" in England and *le diablo* in France, was wildly popular.

The name *diabolo* is traced to French engineer Gustave Phillappart in 1906. Despite the similarity to *diablo* and other language's names for devil, or the history, Phillappart claimed that *diabolo* came from the Greek *dia bolo*, meaning "across throw." If you say so, Gustave!

Plate 30 :

Hats, hats, and more hats! Rather like shoes … a Regency lady can never have too many hats. This woman has her hats displayed on a fabulous rack, and the variety of styles are wonderful.

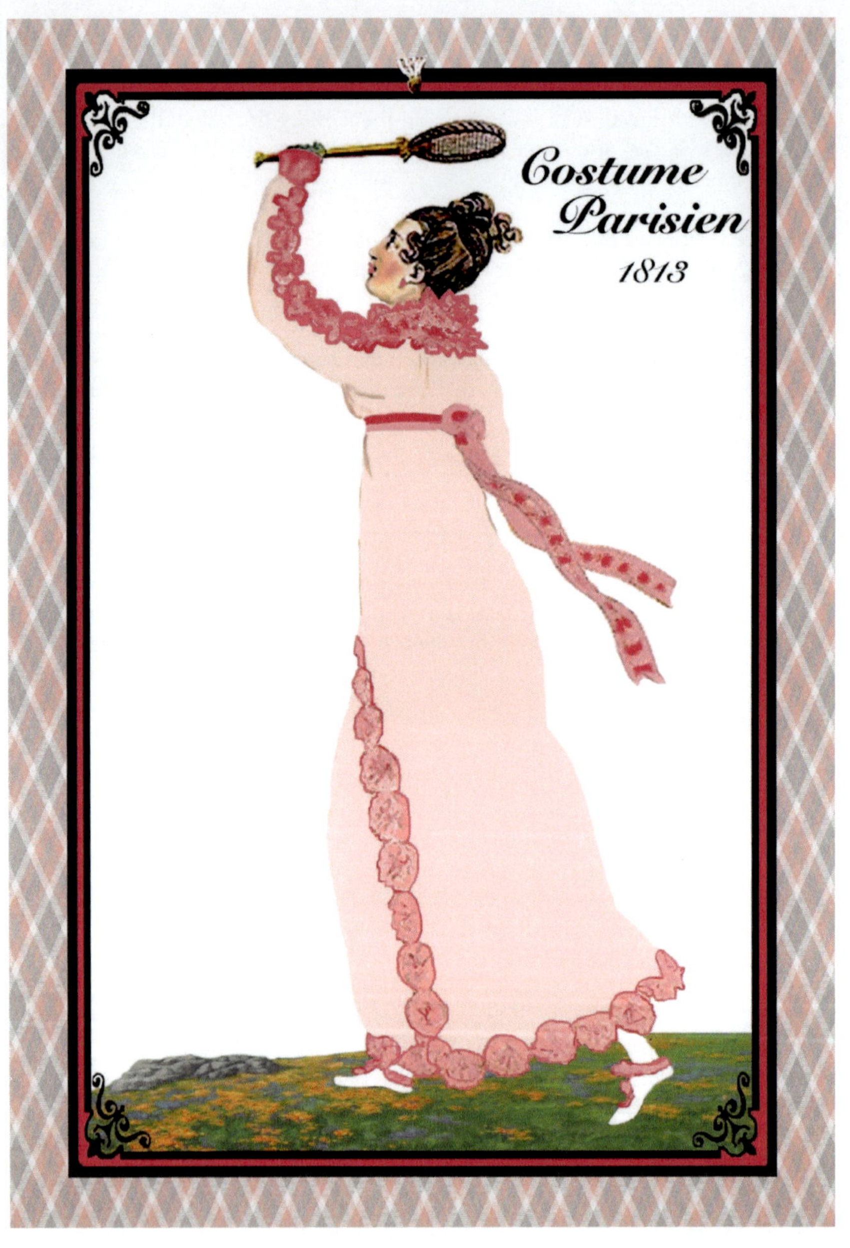

Plate 31

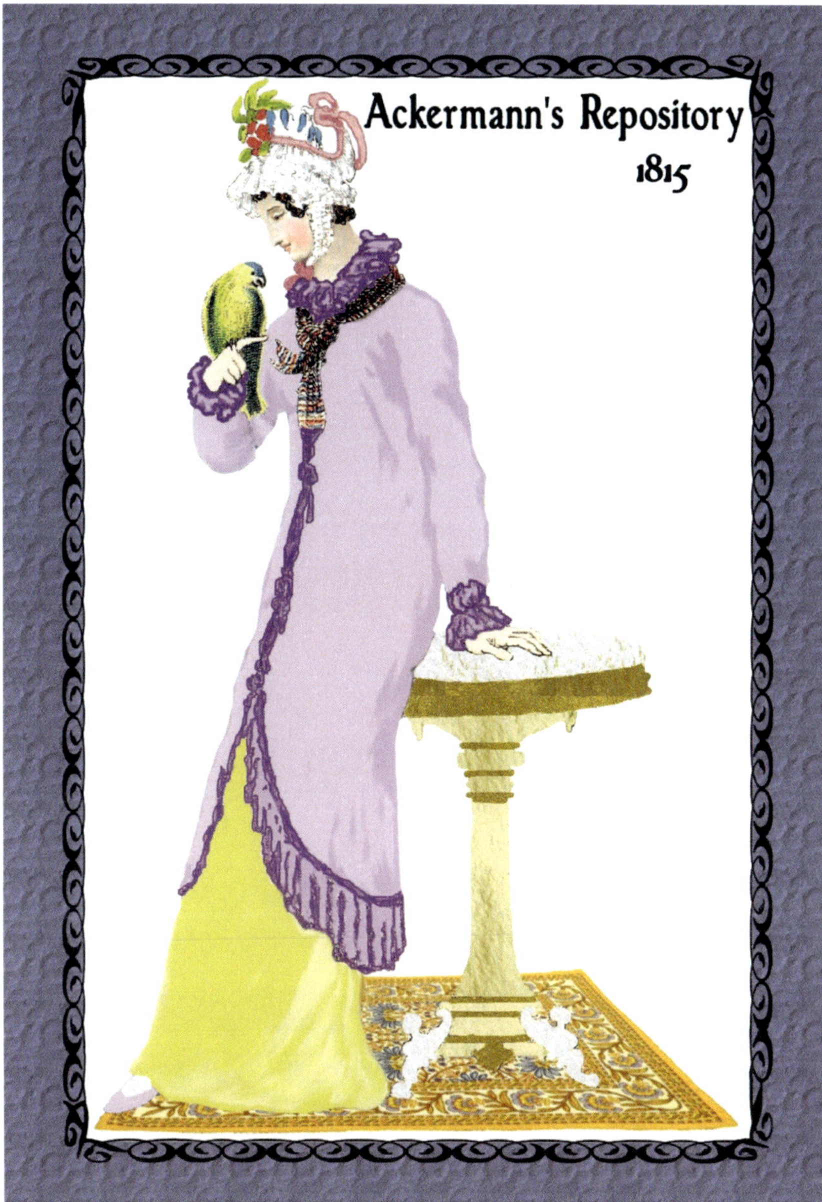

Ackermann's Repository
1815

Plate 32

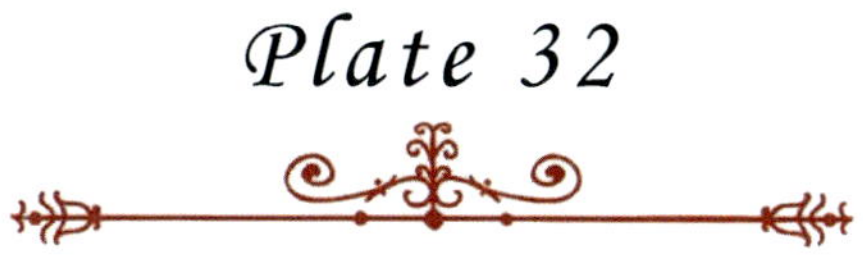

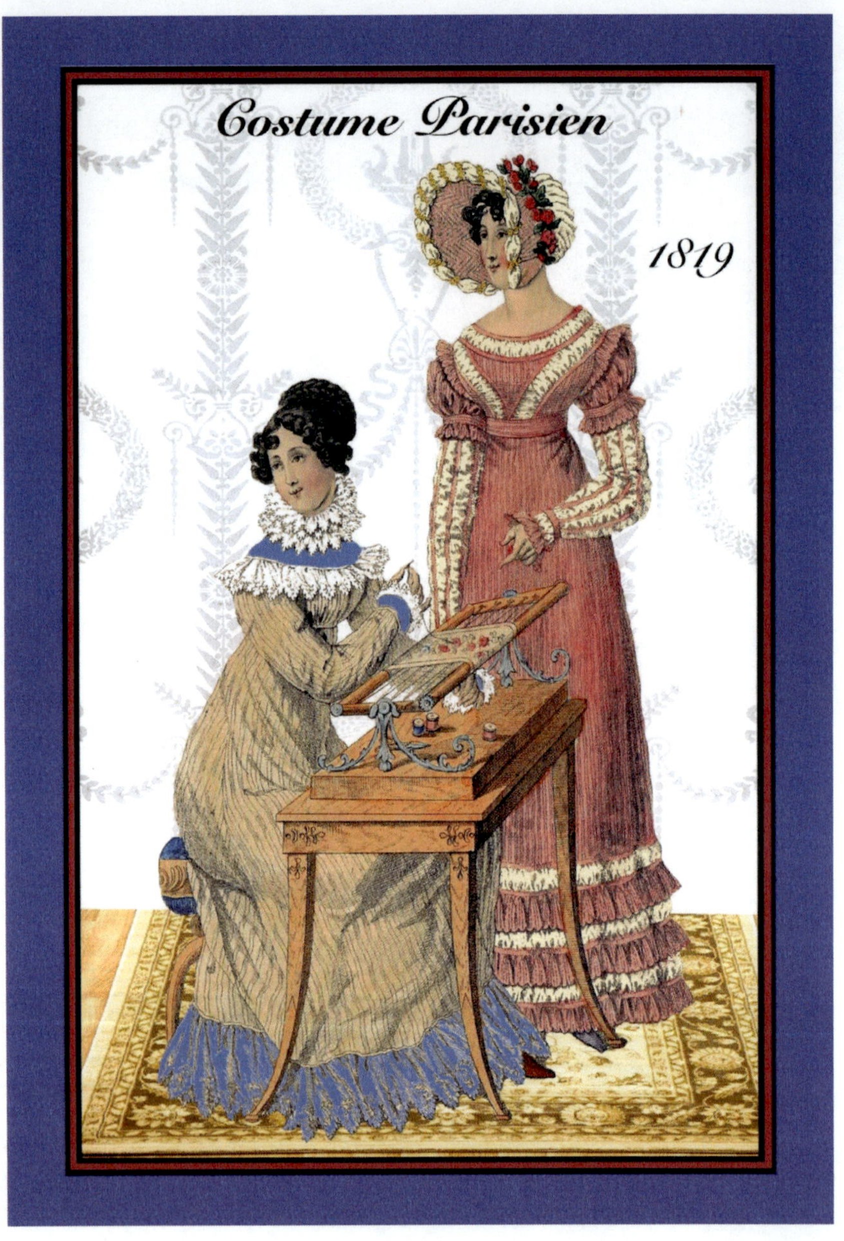

Plate 33

Plate 31 :

Lady wearing a ruffled frock playing "battledore and shuttlecock." The game originated in Greece some 2000 years ago. The path to the streets of England, where it was played by peasant children by the late-16th century, is unknown. What is certain is that from the 17th century onward it was a popular game amongst the upper class. The game rules were simply two people hitting the shuttlecock back and forth with small wooden battledores for as long as possible without falling to the ground. The name "badminton" came from Badminton House, the Duke of Beaufort's residence in Gloucestershire. Why, and precisely when, is a bit of a mystery. However, it is recorded that the game was played at Badminton House, and in the 1860s when the addition of a net or rope dividing line became part of the rules.

Plate 32 :

A lady in a morning dress holding a parrot. Exotic pets were prized acquisitions. I am not a bird-as-pet lover, but my sister has a feathered menagerie, so I can appreciate the unique bond forged between humans and intelligent bird species, such as parrots.

The description in the magazine is as follows: "A loose robe of line cambric or worked jaconet muslin, over a petticoat of the same, flounced with French trimming; long full sleeve, confined at the wrist with treble drawings and ornamented with corresponding trimming. The robe, *negligée*, of demi-length is gathered into a Vandyke ruff, and is worn with a coloured silk handkerchief tied carelessly round the neck. A mob cap, composed of net and Brussels lace, decorated with a cluster of flowers and bows of satin ribbon. Slippers or sandals of pale tan-coloured kid.

Plate 33 :

This third print of women embroidering is unique in two ways. One, as the years advanced toward the 1820s, the waistlines for gowns gradually dropped. Compare the two dresses seen here. The high, Empire level waist was still fashionable (the seated lady) concurrent with designs providing a few more inches of bosom space!

Second, the embroidery frame used here is constructed exactly as described in Plate #26, only on a smaller scale. This type of frame could not be handheld — the table required for stability — and while not large enough for a huge cloth piece, it accommodated fabrics too thick for a tambour hoop and enabled a full view of the project.

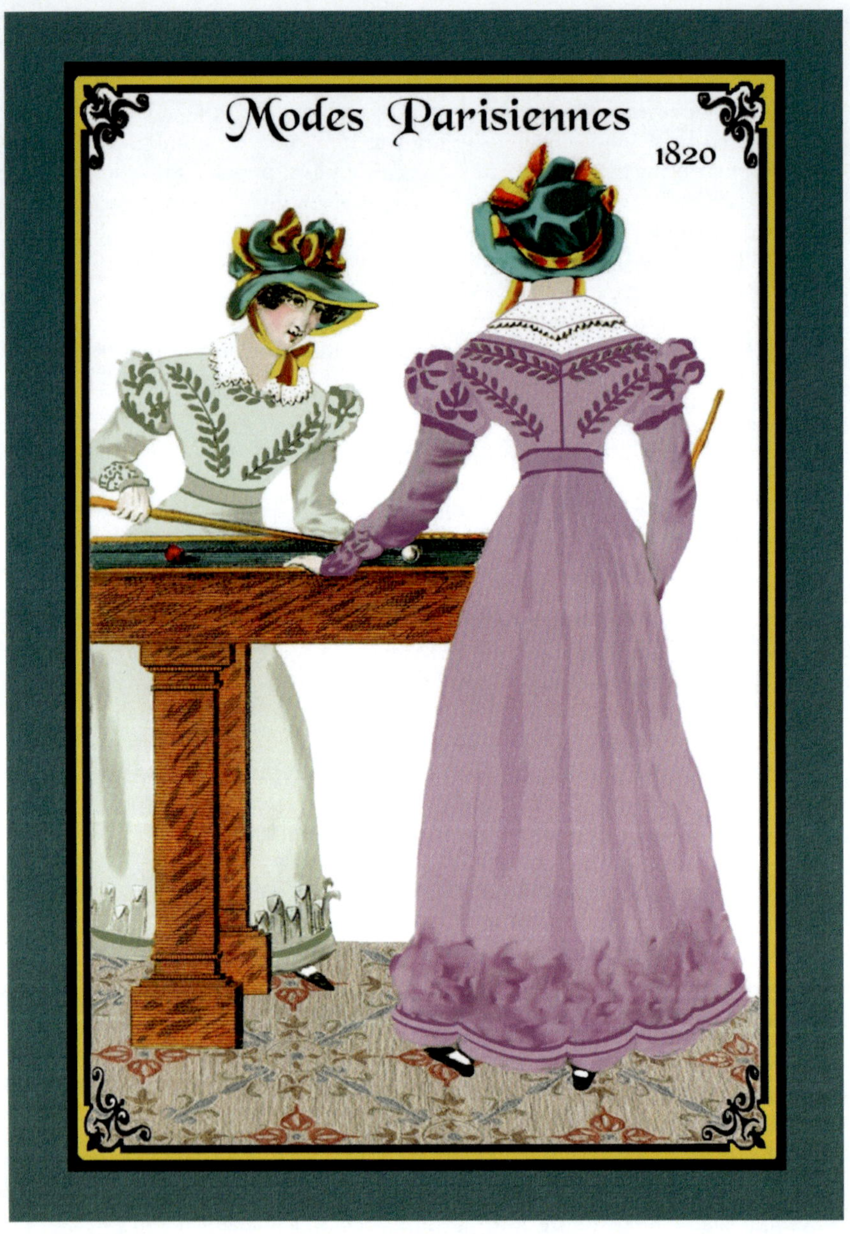

Plate 34

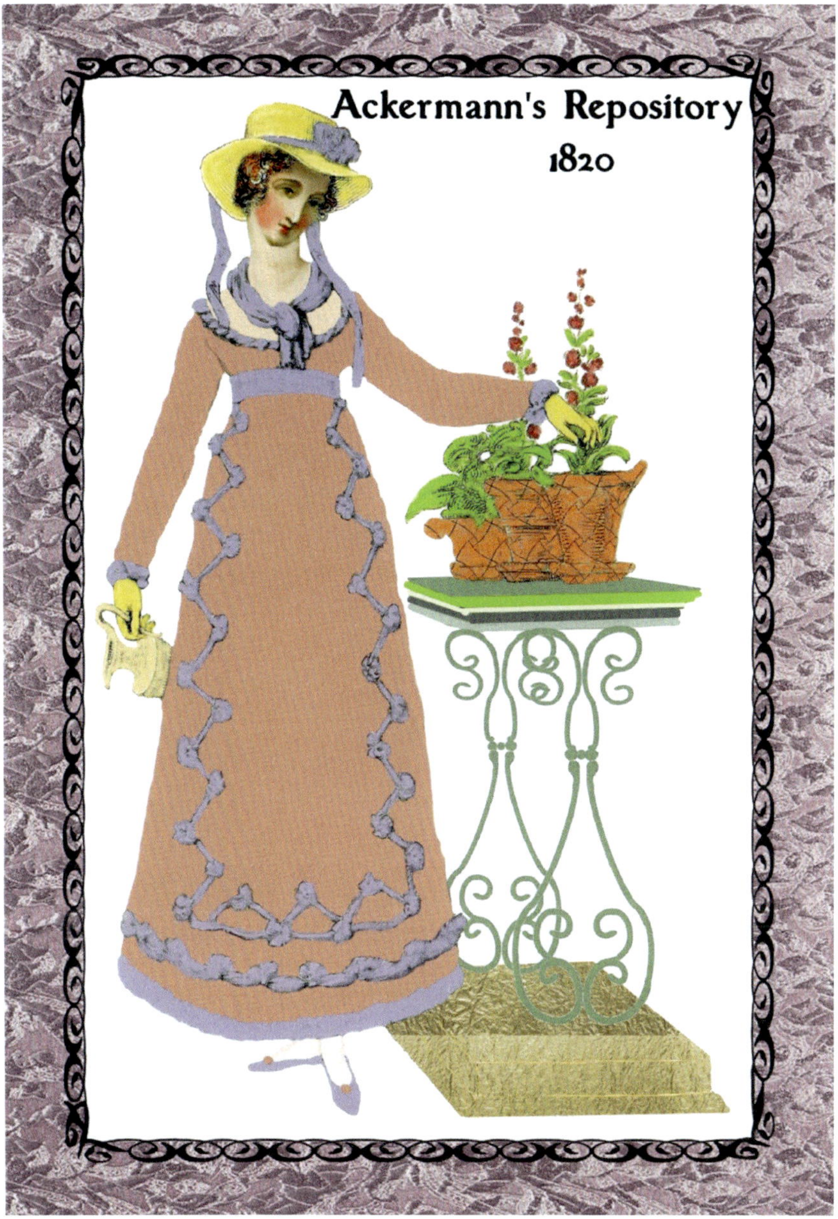

Ackermann's Repository
1820

Plate 35

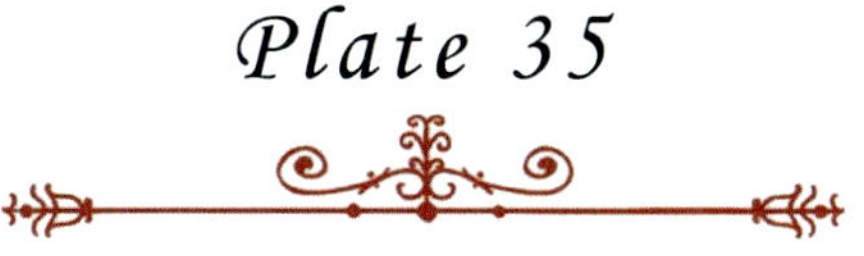

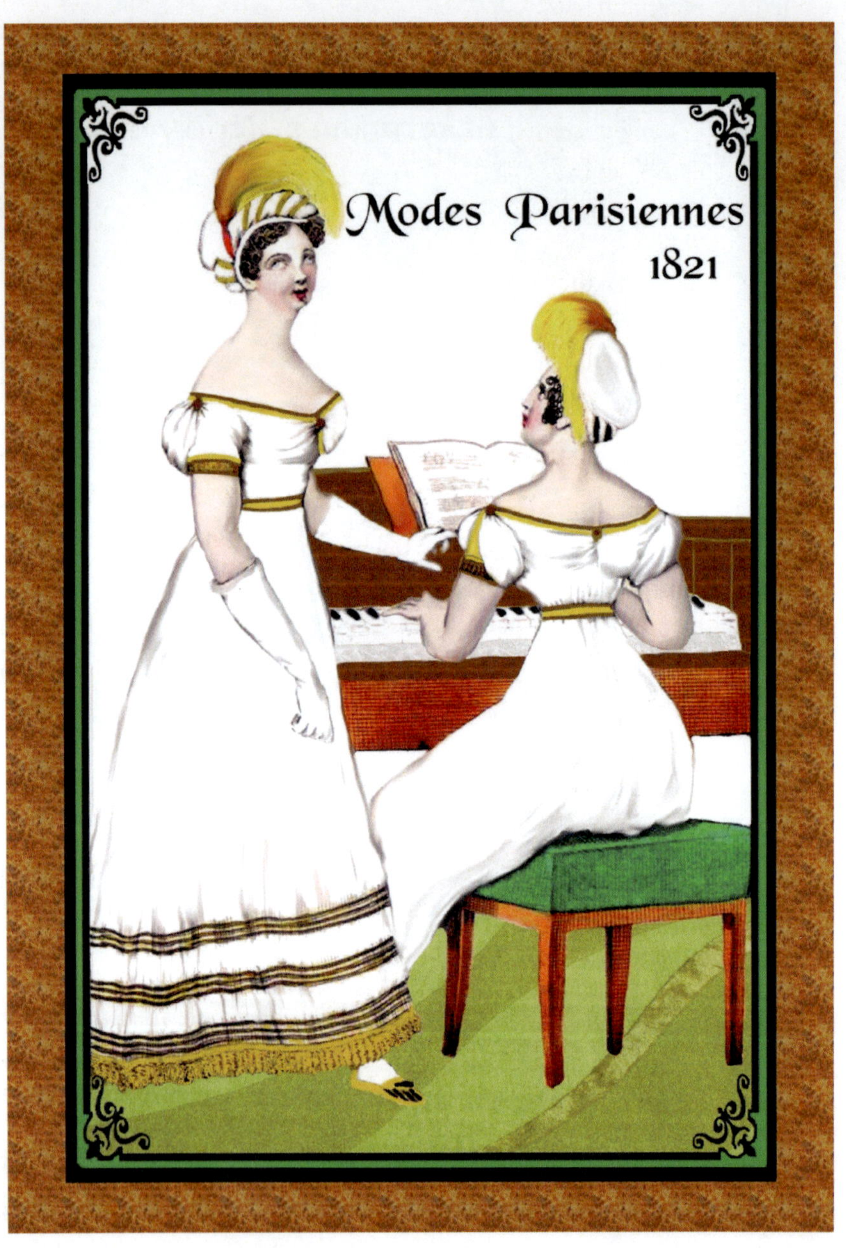

Plate 36

Plate 34 :

Two ladies playing billiards. As a game typically associated with Regency Era gentlemen, this print is extremely cool. English billiards is a game similar to and of the same historical evolution as American pool, but with entirely different rules. However, until the beginning of national standards in 1870, "billiards" was a game played in multiple ways, on a variety of surfaces, with different numbers of balls, using cues or maces, aiming for or avoiding the pockets (called "hazards"), and so on. Whatever rules employed at a given time, billiards was a sport for gentlemen, and, apparently, ladies too!

Plate 35 :

A lady tending to her flowers. This print is amazing for the dress alone. Labeled a "Cottage Dress" on the original Ackermann print, from what I could ascertain the array of names for dresses overlapped and were largely indefinable. One magazine's "full dress" or "carriage dress" was another magazine's "half dress" or "walking dress." In this print, the cottage dress is akin to the usual walking dress, meaning the garment was meant to be worn while outdoors, but in a casual setting.

Whether she is outside, in an orangery, or any other room in her house, growing flowers and even working in the soil of a garden patch was a desirable pastime. An accomplished lady gardener took pride in a home adorned with freshly cut, fragrant flowers touched by her own hand.

Plate 36 :

For the final print, these ladies engaged in a musical duet felt perfect. Mastery with an instrument and vocal prowess, of all the diversions a Regency lady spent time on, was of prime value and importance. The ability to entertain guests, whether in an effort to display one's talents for enticement or merely to be an excellent hostess, was essential.

These ladies — sisters or twins, perhaps — are wearing identical gowns of white gauze, and the waistline is nearly to the natural place on a woman's body. The turban hats with brightly colored feather plumes are outstanding.

A fabulous plate to complete this volume of ***Regency Prints Refined.***

About the Author

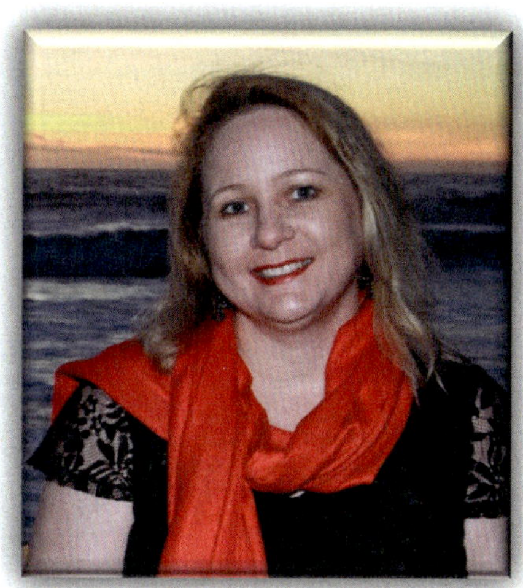

Sharon Lathan is the best-selling author of The Darcy Saga sequel series to Jane Austen's *Pride & Prejudice*. Sharon began writing in 2006 and her first novel, *Mr. and Mrs. Fitzwilliam Darcy: Two Shall Become One* was published in 2009. Sharon's ninth novel - *Darcy & Elizabeth: A Season of Courtship* - is Book One of the Darcy Saga Prequel Duo recounting the betrothal months before the Darcy Saga began. *Miss Darcy Falls in Love* was chosen for World Book Night US 2014.

Sharon is a native Californian relocated in September 2013 to the green hills of Kentucky, where she resides with her husband of twenty-nine-years. Currently retired from a thirty-year profession as a registered nurse in Neonatal Intensive Care, Sharon is pursuing her dream as a full-time writer.

Sharon is a member of the Jane Austen Society of North America, JASNA Greater Louisville Region, the Romance Writers of America, the Beau Monde chapter of the RWA, and the Louisville Romance Writers where she serves as the website designer and manager. Together with novelist Regina Jeffers, Sharon created Austen Authors, a group blog with twenty published authors of Jane Austen inspired literary fiction. Austen Authors website: www.AustenAuthors.com

For more information about Sharon, the Regency Era, and her novels, visit her website/blog at: www.SharonLathanAuthor.com. Sharon is on Facebook as SharonLathanNovelist, Twitter @SharonLathan, and Pinterest as SharonLathan62

The Darcy Saga Series

Happily Ever After Comes True...

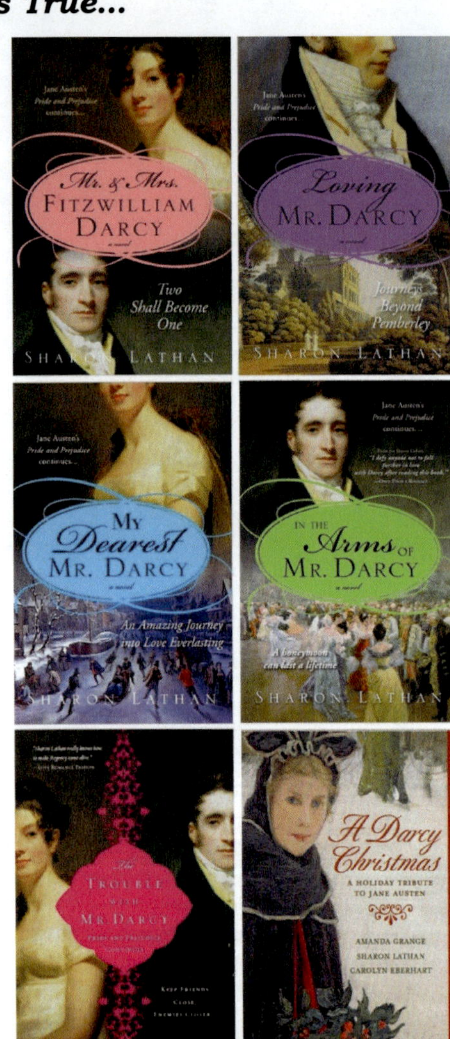

Beginning on their wedding day, Darcy and Elizabeth are two people who are deeply in love with one another and are excited to begin their marriage.

The Darcy Saga sequel series to Jane Austen's *Pride and Prejudice* is a sweetly romantic, historically accurate tale recounting the daily life of newlyweds Mr. and Mrs. Fitzwilliam Darcy. Through five novels and one novella, Sharon Lathan presents a vision of happiness in marriage.

Meet new friends and family members. Delve deeper into familiar characters and their futures. Dwell in the Regency world at Pemberley and London. Through it all, delight in an unparalleled love story with Darcy and Elizabeth.

Mr. and Mrs. Fitzwilliam Darcy: Two Shall Become One

Loving Mr. Darcy: Journeys Beyond Pemberley

My Dearest Mr. Darcy

In The Arms of Mr. Darcy

The Trouble With Mr. Darcy

A Darcy Christmas

"If you enjoy enthusiastic romance passionately written featuring the redoubtable Mr. Darcy and his wife, then "I would by no means suspend any pleasure of yours"!" – ***Austenprose***

Darcy and Elizabeth: A Season of Courtship

Accepting a marriage proposal is merely the beginning...

Readers of The Darcy Saga have shared in the romance, life, and marital escapades of Mr. and Mrs. Darcy. Now the "prequel to the sequel" recounts the weeks in between as two new lovers prepare for happily ever after.

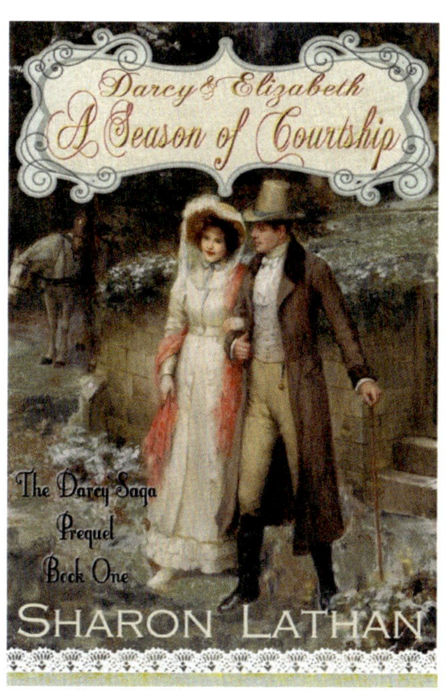

Embark on the journey as Darcy and Elizabeth overcome the rocky past and discover the depth of their love. Delight in budding passion and sweet romance. Enjoy the wedding planning and adventures during the initial weeks of their engagement.

A Season of Courtship promises Hope of the Future.

Darcy and Elizabeth: A Season of Courtship

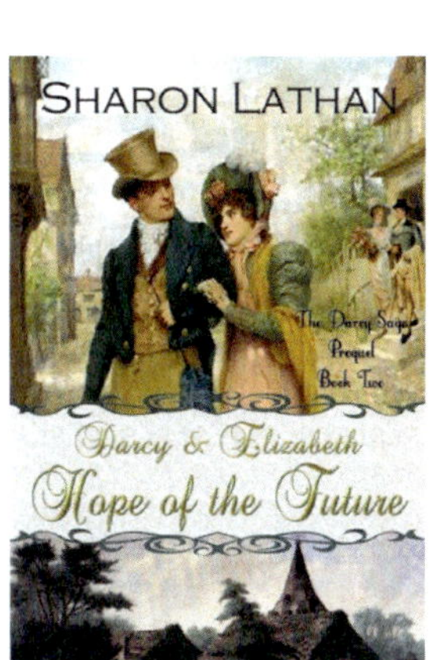

Darcy and Elizabeth: Hope of the Future

The conclusion to the "prequel to the sequel" is a work in progress. Hopefully to be released before the end of 2015.

Miss Darcy Falls in Love

An intimate journey of love, life, and the passionate pursuit of happiness.

Noble young ladies were expected to play an instrument, but societal restrictions would have chafed for Georgiana Darcy, an accomplished musician.

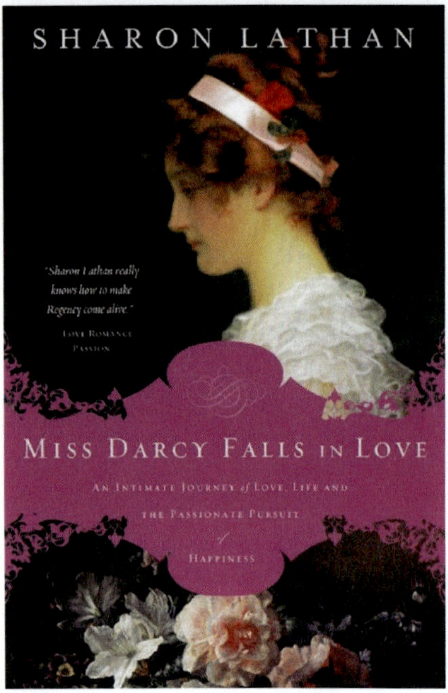

While touring Europe and post-Napoleonic France, Miss Georgiana Darcy discovers her deepest passion: composing and playing music. In Paris she meets two men who augment her passion, fire her soul, spark her sensuality, and fan the flames of her musical inspiration. Yet only one holds the key to her happiness and is her true soul mate.

Amid the backdrop of Paris in this tumultuous time in history, Georgiana must learn to direct her destiny and fully understand her heart.

Miss Darcy Falls in Love

“Sharon Lathan has another home run hit on her hands here. Her name is certainly solidified with what good Jane Austen fan fiction should be. Fast-paced and always full of the romance we all dream about, Miss Darcy Falls in Love is not one you'll want to miss.” ***Austenprose***

“If you are a Jane Austen fan, if you love historical novels, then Ms. Lathan's wonderfully written, vividly detailed, and sweet romance novel will be one that you don't want to miss out on!” ***Romancing the Book***

“This is a story that fully immerses its readers in the world of the characters, from the rainy streets of Lyon and Paris and the quiet hush of the churches and museums Georgiana visits, to the dazzle and splendor of the society balls that light up the evenings.” ***The Romance Reviews***

The Passions of Dr. Darcy

You never know where a life of purpose may lead...

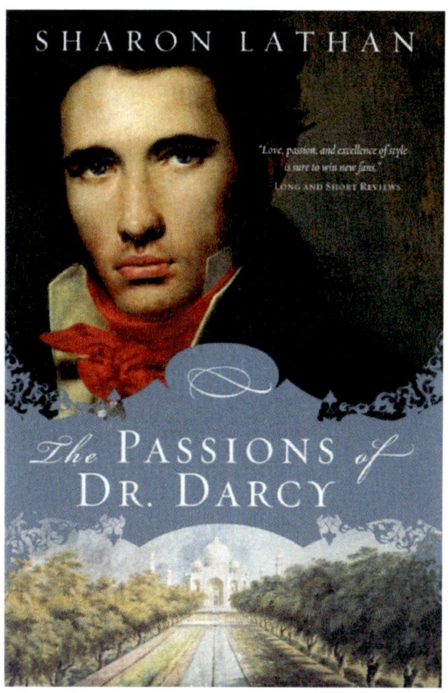

While Fitzwilliam Darcy is enjoying an idyllic childhood at Pemberley, his vibrant and beloved uncle, Dr. George Darcy, becomes one of the most renowned young physicians of the day. Determined to do something more with his life than cater to a spoiled aristocracy, George accepts a post with the British East India Company and travels in search of a life of meaning and purpose.

When George Darcy returns to Pemberley after many years abroad, the drama and heartbreak of his travels offer a fascinating glimpse into a gentleman's journey of self-discovery and romance.

Explore a fascinating and unique aspect of the Regency period, when the British Empire offered the young noblemen of the day promising adventures all over the world.

The Passions of Dr. Darcy

"A splendid tale of one man's determination . . . to be the best in his chosen profession . . . and to find love." ***New York Journal of Books***

"The story is entertaining, especially for those who take pleasure, as I did, in details of 18th-century medicine and learning about the exotic India of this era." ***Historical Novel Society***

"Lathan is an expert in character development. We travel across every reach of the Indian subcontinent for over 30 years with George, exploring its vibrant and rich history and the intriguing characters that he meets along the way. Lathan has made a touching story of a man who finds himself in India. It was a journey which I was happy to take." ***Austenprose***

Made in the USA
Middletown, DE
30 November 2016